T0144326

AWAKENED
IMAGINATION

AWAKENED IMAGINATION

Deluxe Edition

Neville Goddard

Includes a Biographical Essay and Timeline by PEN Award-Winning Historian

Mitch Horowitz

Published 2022 by Gildan Media LLC
aka G&D Media
www.GandDmedia.com

AWAKENED IMAGINATION. Copyright © 2022 G&D Media. All rights reserved

No part of this book may be used, reproduced or transmitted in any manner whatsoever, by any means (electronic, photocopying, recording, or otherwise), without the prior written permission of the author, except in the case of brief quotations embodied in critical articles and reviews. No liability is assumed with respect to the use of the information contained within. Although every precaution has been taken, the author and publisher assume no liability for errors or omissions. Neither is any liability assumed for damages resulting from the use of the information contained herein.

Front cover design by David Rheinhardt of Pyrographx

Library of Congress Cataloging-in-Publication Data is available upon request

ISBN: 978-1-7225-0579-0

10   9   8   7   6   5   4   3   2   1

To Bill

CONTENTS

I

Awakened Imagination
by Neville Goddard
1

II

Chariot of Fire: The Ideas of Neville Goddard
by Mitch Horowitz
79

Neville Goddard Timeline
137

About the Authors
141

I

AWAKENED IMAGINATION

"*Imagination, the real and eternal world of which this Vegetable Universe is but a faint shadow. What is the life of Man but Art and Science?*"

WILLIAM BLAKE, *"JERUSALEM"*

"*Imagination is more important than knowledge.*"

ALBERT EINSTEIN, *ON SCIENCE*

&

1

WHO IS YOUR IMAGINATION?

*"I rest not from my great task
To open the Eternal Worlds, to open the immortal
Eyes Of Man inwards into the Worlds
of Thought: into Eternity
Ever expanding in the Bosom of God,
the Human Imagination."*

BLAKE: "JERUSALEM," 5:18-20

Certain words in the course of long use gather so many strange connotations that they almost cease to mean anything at all. Such a word is 'imagination.' This word is made to serve all manner of ideas, some of them directly opposed to one another. 'Fancy, thought, hallucination, suspicion:' indeed, so wide is its use and so varied its meanings, the word 'imagination' has no status nor fixed significance. For example, we ask a man to 'use his imagination,' meaning that his present outlook is too restricted and therefore not equal to the task. In the next breath we tell him that his ideas are 'pure imagination,' thereby implying that his ideas are unsound. We speak of a jealous or suspicious person as a 'victim of his own imagination,' meaning that his thoughts are untrue. A minute later we pay a man the highest tribute by describing him as a 'man of imagination.' Thus the word imagination has no definite meaning. Even the dictionary gives us no help. It defines imagination as (1) the picturing power or act of the mind, the constructive or creative principle; (2) a phantasm; (3) an irrational notion or belief; (4) planning, plotting or scheming as involving mental construction.

I identify the central figure of the Gospels with human imagination, the power which makes the forgiveness of sins, the achievement of our goals, inevitable.

> "All things were made by him; and without him was
> not anything made that was made."
>
> JOHN 1:3

There is only one thing in the world, Imagination, and all our deformations of it.

> "He is despised and rejected of men; a man of sorrows,
> and acquainted with grief."
>
> ISAIAH 53:3

Imagination is the very gateway of reality. "Man," said Blake, "is either the ark of God or a phantom of the earth and of the water." "Naturally he is only a natural organ subject to Sense." "The Eternal Body of Man is The Imagination: that is God himself, The Divine Body. ישוע: Jesus: we are his Members."

I know of no greater and truer definition of the Imagination than that of Blake. By imagination we have the power to be anything we desire to be. Through imagination we disarm and transform the violence of the world. Our most intimate as well as our most casual relationships become imaginative as we awaken to "the mystery hid from the ages," that Christ in us is our imagination. We then realize that only as we live by imagination can we truly be said to live at all.

I want this book to be the simplest, clearest, frankest work I have the power to make it, that I may encourage you to function imaginatively, that you may open your "Immortal Eyes inwards into the Worlds of Thought," where you behold every desire of your heart as ripe grain "white already to harvest."

> *"I am come that they might have life, and that they*
> *might have it more abundantly."*
>
> JOHN 10:10

The abundant life that Christ promised us is ours to experience *now*, but not until we have the sense of Christ *as our imagination* can we experience it.

> *"The mystery hid from the ages . . . Christ in you, the*
> *hope of glory."*
>
> COLOSSIANS 1:26

is your imagination. This is the mystery which I am ever striving to realize more keenly myself and to urge upon others.

Imagination is our redeemer, "the Lord from Heaven" born of man but not begotten of man.

Every man is Mary and birth to Christ must give. If the story of the immaculate conception and birth of Christ appears irrational to man, it is only because it is misread as biography, history and cosmology, and the modern explorers of the imagination do not help by calling It the unconscious or subconscious mind. Imagination's birth and growth is the gradual transition from a God of tradition to a God of experience. If the birth of Christ in man seems slow, it is only because man is unwilling to let go the comfortable but false anchorage of tradition.

When imagination is discovered as the first principle of religion, the stone of literal understanding will have felt the rod of Moses and, like the rock of Zin, issue forth the water of psychological meaning to quench the thirst of humanity; and all who take the proffered cup and live a life according to this truth, will transform the water of psychological meaning into the wine of forgiveness. Then, like the good Samaritan, they will pour it on the wounds of all.

The Son of God is not to be found in history nor in any external form. He can only be found as the imagination of him in whom His presence becomes manifest.

> "O would thy heart but be a manger for His birth! God would once more become a child on earth."

Man is the garden in which this only begotten Son of God sleeps. He awakens this Son by lifting his imagination up to heaven and clothing men in godlike stature. We must go on imagining better than the best we know.

Man in the moment of his awakening to the imaginative life must meet the test of Sonship.

> "Father, reveal Thy Son in me" and
> "It pleased God to reveal His Son in me."
>
> GALATIANS 1:16

The supreme test of Sonship is the forgiveness of sin. The test that your imagination is Christ Jesus, the Son of God, is your ability to forgive sin. Sin means missing one's mark in life, falling short of one's ideal, failing to achieve one's aim. Forgiveness means identification of man with his ideal or aim in life. This is the work of awakened imagination, the supreme work, for it tests man's ability to enter into and partake of the nature of his opposite.

> "Let the weak man say, I am strong."
>
> JOEL 3:10

Reasonably this is impossible. Only awakened imagination can enter into and partake of the nature of its opposite.

This conception of Christ Jesus as human imagination raises these fundamental questions. Is imagination a power sufficient, not merely to enable me to assume that I am strong, but is it also of itself capable of executing the idea? Suppose that I desire to be in some other place or situation. Could I, by imagining myself into such a state and place, bring about their physical realization? Suppose I could not afford the journey and suppose my present social and financial status oppose the idea that I want to realize. Would imagination be sufficient of itself to incarnate these desires? Does imagination comprehend reason? By reason I mean deductions from the observations of the senses. Does it recognize the external world of facts? In the practical way of every-day life is imagination a complete guide to behaviour? Suppose I am capable of acting with continuous imagination, that is, suppose I am capable of sustaining the feeling of my wish fulfilled, will my assumption harden into fact? And, if it does harden into fact, shall I on reflection find that my actions through the period of incubation have been reasonable? Is my imagination a power sufficient, not merely to assume the feeling of the wish fulfilled, but is it also of itself capable of incarnating the idea? After assuming that I am already what I want to be, must I continually guide myself by reasonable ideas and actions in order to bring about the fulfillment of my assumption?

Experience has convinced me that an assumption, though false, if persisted in will harden into fact, that continuous imagination is sufficient for all things and all my reasonable plans and actions will never make up for my lack of continuous imagination.

Is it not true that the teachings of the Gospels can only be received in terms of faith and that the Son of God is constantly looking for signs of faith in people, that is, faith in their own imagination? Is not the promise

"Believe that ye receive and ye shall receive."

MARK 11:24

the same as "Imagine that you are and you shall be"? Was it not an imaginary state in which Moses

"Endured, as seeing him who is invisible"?

HEBREWS 11:27

Was it not by the power of his own imagination that he endured?

Truth depends upon the intensity of the imagination not upon external facts. Facts are the fruit bearing witness of the use or misuse of the imagination. Man becomes what he imagines. He has a self-determined history. Imagination is the way, the truth, the life revealed. We cannot get hold of truth with the logical mind. Where the natural man of sense sees a bud, imagination sees a rose full-blown. Truth cannot be encompassed by facts. As we awaken to the imaginative life we discover that to imagine a thing is so makes it so, that a true judgment need not conform to the external reality to which it relates.

The imaginative man does not deny the reality of the sensuous outer world of Becoming, but he knows that it is the inner world of continuous Imagination that is the force by which the sensuous outer world of Becoming is brought to pass. He sees the outer world and all its happenings as projections of the inner world of Imagination. To him everything is a manifestation of the mental activity which goes on in man's imagination without the sensuous reasonable man being aware of it. But he realizes that every man must become conscious of this inner activity and see the relationship between the inner causal world of imagination and the sensuous outer world of effects.

It is a marvelous thing to find that you can imagine yourself into the state of your fulfilled desire and escape from the jails which ignorance built.

The Real Man is a Magnificent Imagination. It is this *self* that must be awakened.

> *"Awake thou that sleepest, and arise from the dead, and Christ shall give thee light."*
>
> EPHESIANS 5:14

The moment man discovers that his imagination is Christ he accomplishes acts which on this level can only be called miraculous. But until man has the sense of Christ *as his imagination*

> *"You did not choose me, I have chosen you"*
>
> JOHN 15:16

he will see everything in pure objectivity without any subjective relationship. Not realizing that all that he encounters is part of himself, he rebels at the thought that he has chosen the conditions of his life, that they are related by affinity to his own mental activity. Man must firmly come to believe that reality lies within him and not without.

Although others have bodies, a life of their own, their reality is rooted in you, ends in you, as yours ends in God.

2

SEALED INSTRUCTIONS

*"The first power that meets us at the threshold of
the soul's domain is the power of imagination."*
DR. FRANZ HARTMANN

I was first made conscious of the power, nature and redemptive function of imagination through the teachings of my friend Abdullah; and through subsequent experiences I learned that Jesus was a symbol of the coming of imagination to man, that the test of His birth in man was the individual's ability to forgive sin; that is, his ability to identify himself or another with his aim in life.

Without the identification of man with his aim the forgiveness of sin is an impossibility, and only the Son of God can forgive sin. Therefore man's ability to identify himself with his aim, though reason and his senses deny it, is proof of the birth of Christ in him. To passively surrender to appearances and bow before the evidence of facts is to confess that Christ is not yet born in you.

Although this teaching shocked and repelled me at first—for I was a convinced and earnest Christian, and did not then know that Christianity could not be inherited by the mere accident of birth but must be consciously adopted as a way of life,—it stole later on, through visions, mystical revelations and practical experiences, into my understanding and found its interpretation in a deeper mood. But I must confess that it is a trying time when those things are shaken which one has always taken for granted.

> *"Seest thou these great buildings? There shall not be left*
> *one stone upon another that shall not be thrown down."*
>
> MARK 13:2

Not one stone of literal understanding will be left after one drinks the water of psychological meaning. All that has been built up by natural religion is cast into the flames of mental fire. Yet, what better way is there to understand Christ Jesus than to identify the central character of the Gospels with human imagination—knowing that every time you exercise your imagination lovingly on behalf of another you are literally mediating God to man and thereby feeding and clothing Christ Jesus, and that whenever you imagine evil against another you are literally beating and crucifying Christ Jesus? Every imagination of man is either the cup of cold water or the sponge of vinegar to the parched lips of Christ.

> *"Let none of you imagine evil in your hearts against his*
> *neighbor"*

warned the prophet Zechariah. When man heeds this advice he will awake from the imposed sleep of Adam into the full consciousness of the Son of God. He is in the world and the world is made by him and the world knows him not: Human Imagination.

I asked myself many times "If my imagination is Christ Jesus and all things are possible to Christ Jesus, are all things possible to me?"

Through experience I have come to know that when I identify myself with my aim in life, then Christ is awake in me.

Christ is sufficient for all things.

> "I lay down my life that I might take it again. No man taketh it from me but I lay it down of myself."
>
> JOHN 10:18

What a comfort it is to know that all that I experience is the result of my own standard of beliefs; that I am the center of my own web of circumstances and that as I change so must my outer world!

The world presents different appearances according as our states of consciousness differ. What we see when we are identified with a state cannot be seen when we are no longer fused with it. By state is meant all that man believes and consents to as true. No idea presented to the mind can realize itself unless the mind accepts it. It depends on the acceptance, the state with which we are identified, how things present themselves. In the fusion of imagination and states is to be found the shaping of the world as it seems. The world is a revelation of the states with which imagination is fused. It is the state *from* which we think that determines the objective world in which we live. The rich man, the poor man, the good man, the thief, are what they are by virtue of the states *from* which they view the world. On the distinction between these states depends the distinction between the worlds of these men. Individually so different is this same world. It is not the actions and behavior of the good man that should be matched but his point of view. Outer reforms are useless if the inner state is not changed. Success is gained not by imitating the outer actions of the successful but by right inner actions and inner talking.

If we detach ourselves from a state, and we may at any moment, the conditions and circumstances to which that union gave being vanish.

It was in the fall of 1933 in New York City that I approached Abdullah with a problem. He asked me one simple question, "What do you want?" I told him that I would like to spend the winter in Barbados, but that I was broke. I literally did not have a nickel.

"If you will imagine yourself to be *in* Barbados," said he, "thinking and viewing the world *from* that state of consciousness instead of thinking *of* Barbados, you will spend the winter there. You must not concern yourself with the ways and means of getting there, for the state of consciousness of already being in Barbados, if occupied by your imagination, will devise the means best suited to realize itself."

Man lives by committing himself to invisible states, by fusing his imagination with what he knows to be other than himself, and in this union he experiences the results of that fusion. No one can lose what he has save by detachment from the state where the things experienced have their natural life.

"You must imagine yourself right into the state of your fulfilled desire," Abdullah told me, "and fall asleep viewing the world from Barbados."

The world which we describe from observation must be as we describe it relative to ourselves. Our imagination connects us with the state desired. But we must use imagination masterfully, not as an onlooker thinking *of* the end, but as a partaker thinking *from* the end. We must actually *be* there in imagination. If we do this, our subjective experience will be realized objectively.

"This is not mere fancy," said he, "but a truth you can prove by experience."

His appeal to enter *into* the wish fulfilled was the secret of thinking *from* the end. Every state is already there as "mere possibility" as long as you think *of* it, but is overpoweringly real when you think *from* it. Thinking from the end is the way of Christ.

I began right there and then fixing my thoughts beyond the limits of sense, beyond that aspect to which my present state gave being, towards the feeling of already being *in* Barbados and viewing the world *from* that standpoint.

He emphasized the importance of the state *from* which man views the world as he falls asleep. All prophets claim that the voice of God is chiefly heard by man in dreams.

> *"In a dream, in a vision of the night, when deep sleep*
> *falleth upon men, in slumberings upon the bed; then he*
> *openeth the ears of men, and sealeth their instruction."*
>
> JOB 33:15:16

That night and for several nights thereafter I fell asleep in the assumption that I was in my father's house in Barbados. Within a month I received a letter from my brother saying that he had a strong desire to have the family together at Christmas and asking me to use the enclosed steamship ticket for Barbados. I sailed two days after I received my brother's letter and spent a wonderful winter in Barbados.

This experience has convinced me that man can be anything he pleases if he will make the conception habitual and think *from* the end. It has also shown me that I can no longer excuse myself by placing the blame on the world of external things—that my good and my evil have no dependency except from myself—that it depends on the state *from* which I view the world how things present themselves.

Man who is free in his choice acts from conceptions which he freely, though not always wisely, chooses. All conceivable states are awaiting our choice and occupancy, but no amount of rationalizing will of itself yield us the state of consciousness which is the only thing worth having.

The imaginative image is the only thing to seek.

The ultimate purpose of imagination is to create in us "the spirit of Jesus," which is continual forgiveness of sin, continual identification of man with his ideal. Only by identifying ourselves with our aim can we forgive ourselves for having missed it. All else is labor in vain. On this path, to whatever place or state we convey our imagination to that place or state we will gravitate physically also.

> *"In my Father's house are many mansions; if it were*
> *not so, I would have told you. I go to prepare a place for*
> *you. And if I go and prepare a place for you, I will come*
> *again, and receive you unto myself; that where I am*
> *there ye may be also."*

> JOHN 14:2

By sleeping in my father's house in my imagination as though I slept there in the flesh, I fused my imagination with that state and was compelled to experience that state in the flesh also.

So vivid was this state to me I could have been seen in my father's house had any sensitive entered the room where in imagination I was sleeping. A man can be seen where in imagination he is, for a man must be where his imagination is, for his imagination is himself. This I know from experience for I have been seen by a few to whom I desired to be seen, when physically I was hundreds of miles away.

I, by the intensity of my imagination and feeling, imagining and feeling myself to be *in* Barbados instead of merely thinking *of* Barbados, had spanned the vast Atlantic to influence my brother into desiring my presence to complete the family circle at Christmas.

Thinking *from* the end, from the feeling of my wish fulfilled, was the source of everything that happened as outer cause, such as my brother's impulse to send me a steamship ticket; and it was also the cause of everything that appeared as results.

In "Ideas of Good and Evil" (Page 35) W. B. Yeats having described a few experiences similar to this experience of mine writes:

> *"If all who have described events like this have not dreamed, we should rewrite our histories, for all men, certainly all imaginative men, must be forever casting forth enchantments, glamour, illusions; and all men, especially tranquil men who have no powerful egotistic life, must be continually passing under their power."*

Determined imagination, thinking *from* the end, is the beginning of all miracles.

I would like to give you an immense belief in miracles, but a miracle is only the name given by those who have no knowledge of the power and function of imagination to the works of imagination. Imagining oneself into the feeling of the wish fulfilled is the means by which a new state is entered. This gives the state the quality of is-ness. Hermes tells us:

> *"That which is, is manifested; that which has been or shall be, is unmanifested, but not dead; for Soul, the eternal activity of God, animates all things."*

The future must become the present in the imagination of the one who would wisely and consciously create circumstances. We must translate vision into Being, thinking *of* into thinking *from*. Imagination must center itself in some state and view the world *from* that state. Thinking *from* the end is an intense perception of the world of fulfilled desire. Thinking *from* the state desired is creative living. Ignorance of this ability to think *from* the end is bondage. It is the root of all bondage with which man is bound. To passively surrender to the evidence of the senses under-estimates the capacities of the Inner Self. Once man accepts thinking *from* the end as a creative principle in which he can cooperate, then he is redeemed from the absurdity of ever attempting to achieve his objective by merely thinking *of* it.

Construct all ends according to the pattern of fulfilled desire.

The whole of life is just the appeasement of hunger, and the infinite states of consciousness from which a man can view the world are purely a means of satisfying that hunger. The principle upon which each state is organized is some form of hunger to lift the passion for self-gratification to ever higher and higher levels of experience. Desire is the mainspring of the mental machinery. It is a blessed thing. It is a right and natural craving which has a state of consciousness as its right and natural satisfaction.

> *"But one thing I do, forgetting the things which are behind, and stretching forward to the things which are before, I press on toward the goal."*

PHILIPPIANS 3:13

It is necessary to have an aim in life. Without an aim we drift. "What wantest thou of me?" is the implied question asked most often by the central figure of the Gospels. In defining your aim you must want it.

> "As the hart panteth after the water brooks, so panteth
> my soul after thee, O God."
>
> PSALMS 42:1

It is lack of this passionate direction to life that makes man fail of accomplishment.

The spanning of the bridge between desire—thinking *of*—and satisfaction—thinking *from*—is all-important. We must move mentally from thinking *of* the end to thinking *from* the end. This, reason could never do. By its nature it is restricted to the evidence of the senses; but imagination, having no such limitation, can. Desire exists to be gratified in the activity of imagination. Through imagination man escapes from the limitation of the senses and the bondage of reason.

There is no stopping the man who can think *from* the end. Nothing can stop him. He creates the means and grows his way out of limitation into ever greater and greater mansions of the Lord. It does not matter what he has been or what he is. All that matters is 'what does he want'? He knows that the world is a manifestation of the mental activity which goes on within himself, so he strives to determine and control the ends *from* which he thinks. In his imagination he dwells in the end, confident that he shall dwell there in the flesh also. He puts his whole trust in the feeling of the wish fulfilled and lives by committing himself to that state, for the art of fortune is to tempt him so to do. Like the man at the pool of Bethesda, he is ready for the moving of the waters of imagination. Knowing that every desire is ripe grain to him who knows how to think *from* the end, he is indifferent to mere reasonable probability and confident that through continuous imagination his assumptions will harden into fact.

But how to persuade men everywhere that thinking *from* the end is the only living, how to foster it in every activity of man, how to reveal it as the plenitude of life and not the compensation of the disappointed: that is the problem.

Life is a controllable thing. You can experience what you please once you realize that you are His Son, and that you are what you are by virtue of the state of consciousness *from* which you think and view the world,

> *"Son, thou art ever with me, and all that I have is thine."*
>
> LUKE 15:31

3

HIGHWAYS OF THE INNER WORLD

"And the children struggled within her ...
and the Lord said unto her, two nations are
in thy womb, and two manner of people shall
be separated from thy bowels; and the one
people shall be stronger than the other people;
and the elder shall serve the younger."

GENESIS 25:22-23

Duality is an inherent condition of life. Everything that exists is double. Man is a dual creature with contrary principles embedded in his nature. They war within him and present attitudes to life which are antagonistic. This conflict is the eternal enterprise, the war in heaven, the neverending struggle of the younger or inner man of imagination to assert His supremacy over the elder or outer man of sense.

"The first shall be last and the last shall be first."

MATTHEW 19:30

"He it is, who coming after me is preferred before me."

JOHN 1:27

"The second man is the Lord from heaven."

I COR. 15:47

Man begins to awake to the imaginative life the moment he feels the presence of another being in himself.

"In your limbs lie nations twain, rival races from their
birth; one the mastery shall gain, the younger o'er the
elder reign."

There are two distinct centers of thought or outlooks on the world possessed by every man. The Bible speaks of these two outlooks as natural and spiritual.

"The natural man receiveth not the things of the spirit
of God: for they are foolishness unto him: neither can
he know them, because they are spiritually discerned."

I CORINTHIANS 2:14

Man's inner body is as real in the world of subjective experience as his outer physical body is real in the world of external realities, but the inner body expresses a more fundamental part of reality. This existing inner body of man must be consciously exercised and directed. The inner world of thought and feeling to which the inner body is attuned has its real structure and exists in its own higher space.

There are two kinds of movement, one that is according to the inner body and another that is according to the outer body. The movement which is according to the inner body is causal, but the outer movement is under compulsion. The inner movement determines the outer which is joined to it, bringing into the outer a movement that is similar to the actions of the inner body. Inner movement is the force by which all events are brought to pass. Outer movement is subject to the compulsion applied to it by the movement of the inner body.

Whenever the actions of the inner body match the actions which the outer must take to appease desire, that desire will be realized.

Construct mentally a drama which implies that your desire is realized and make it one which involves movement of self. Immobilize your outer physical self. Act precisely as though you were going to take a nap, and start the predetermined action in imagination. A vivid representation of the action is the beginning of that action. Then, as you are falling asleep, consciously imagine yourself into the scene. The length of the sleep is not important, a short nap is sufficient, but carrying the action into sleep thickens fancy into fact.

At first your thoughts may be like rambling sheep that have no shepherd. Don't despair. Should your attention stray seventy times seven, bring it back seventy times seven to its predetermined course until from sheer exhaustion it follows the appointed path.

The inner journey must never be without direction. When you take to the inner road it is to do what you did mentally before you started. You go for the prize you have already seen and accepted.

In The Road to Xanadu (P. 103) Professor John Livingston Lowes says:

> *"But I have long had the feeling, which this study has matured to a conviction, that Fancy and Imagination are not two powers at all, but one. The valid distinction which exists between them lies, not in the materials with which they operate, but in the degree of intensity of the operant power itself. Working at high tension the imaginative energy assimilates and transmutes; keyed low, the same energy aggregates and yokes together those images which at its highest pitch, it merges indissolubly into one."*

Fancy assembles, imagination fuses.

Here is a practical application of this theory. A year ago a blind girl living in the city of San Francisco found herself confronted with a transportation problem. A rerouting of buses forced her to make three transfers between her home and her office. This lengthened her trip from fifteen minutes to two hours and fifteen minutes. She thought seriously about this problem and came to the decision that a car was the solution. She knew that she could not drive a car but felt that she could be driven in one. Putting this theory to the test that 'whenever the actions of the inner self correspond to the actions which the outer physical self must take to appease desire, that desire will be realized,' she said to herself "I will sit here and imagine that I am being driven to my office."

Sitting in her living room she began to imagine herself seated in a car. She felt the rhythm of the motor. She imagined that she smelled the odor of gasoline, felt the motion of the car, touched the sleeve of the driver and felt that the driver was a man. She felt the car stop, and turning to her companion, said "Thank you very much, sir." To which he replied, "The pleasure is all mine." Then she stepped from the car and heard the door snap shut as she closed it.

She told me that she centered her imagination on being *in* a car and although blind viewed the city from her imaginary ride. She did not think *of* the ride. She thought *from* the ride and all that *it* implied. This controlled and subjectively directed purposive ride raised her imagination to its full potency. She kept her purpose ever before her, knowing there was cohesion in purposive inner movement. In these mental journeys an emotional continuity must be sustained—the emotion of fulfilled desire. Expectancy and desire were so intensely joined that they passed at once from a mental state into a physical act.

The inner self moves along the predetermined course best when the emotions collaborate. The inner self must be fired, and it is best fired by the thought of great deeds and personal gain. We must take pleasure in our actions.

On two successive days the blind girl took her imaginary ride, giving it all the joy and sensory vividness of reality. A few hours after her second imaginary ride a friend told her of a story in the evening paper. It was a story of a man who was interested in the blind. The blind girl phoned him and stated her problem. The very next day, on his way home, he stopped in at a bar and while there had the urge to tell the story of the blind girl to his friend the proprietor. A total stranger, on hearing the story, volunteered to drive the blind girl home every day. The man who told the story then said, "If you will take her home, I will take her to work."

This was over a year ago, and since that day this blind girl has been driven to and from her office by these two gentlemen. Now, instead of spending two hours and fifteen minutes on three buses, she is at her office in less than fifteen minutes. And on that first ride to her office she turned to her good Samaritan and said, "Thank you very much, sir"; and he replied, "The pleasure is all mine."

Thus, the objects of her imagination were to her the realities of which the physical manifestation was only the witness. The determinative animating principle was the imaginative ride. Her triumph could be a surprise only to those who did not know of her inner ride. She mentally viewed the world from this imaginative ride with such a clearness of vision that every aspect of the city attained identity. These inner movements not only produce corresponding outer movements: this is the law which operates beneath all physical appearances. He who practices these exercises of bi-location will develop unusual powers of concentration and quiescence and will inevitably achieve waking consciousness on the inner and dimensionally larger world. Actualizing strongly she fulfilled her desire, for viewing the city *from* the feeling of her wish fulfilled, she matched the state desired and granted that to herself which sleeping men ask of God.

To realize your desire an action must start in your imagination, apart from the evidence of the senses, involving movement of self and implying fulfillment of your desire. Whenever it is the action which the outer self takes to appease desire, that desire will be realized.

The movement of every visible object is caused not by things outside the body but by things within it which operate from within outward. The journey is in yourself. You travel along the highways of the inner world. Without inner movement it is impossible to bring forth anything. Inner action is introverted sensation. If you will construct mentally a drama which implies that you have realized your objective, then close your eyes and drop your thoughts inward, centering your imagination all the while in the predetermined action and partake in that action, you will become a self-determined being.

Inner action orders all things according to the nature of itself. Try it and see whether a desirable ideal once formulated is possible, for only by this process of experiment can you realize your potentialities. It is thus that this creative principle is being realized. So the clue to purposive living is to center your imagination in the action and feeling of fulfilled desire with such awareness, such sensitiveness, that you initiate and experience movement upon the inner world.

Ideas only act if they are felt, if they awaken inner movement. Inner movement is conditioned by self-motivation, outer movement by compulsion.

> *"Wherever the sole of your foot shall tread, the same give I unto you."*
>
> JOSHUA 1:3

and remember

> *"The Lord thy God in the midst of thee is mighty."*
>
> ZEPHANIAH 3:17

4

THE PRUNING SHEARS
OF REVISION

"The second man is the Lord from heaven"
I CORINTHIANS 15:47

"Never will he say caterpillars. He'll say, 'There's
a lot of butterflies-as-is-to-be on our cabbages,
Prue.' He won't say 'It's winter.' He'll say,
'Summer's sleeping.' And there's no bud little
enough nor sad-coloured enough for Kester
not to callen it the beginnings of the blow."
MARY WEBB. (PRECIOUS BANE)

The very first act of correction or cure is always 'revise.' One must start with oneself. It is one's attitude that must be changed.

"What we are, that only can we see."

EMERSON

It is a most healthy and productive exercise to daily relive the day as you wish you had lived it, revising the scenes to make them conform to your ideals. For instance, suppose today's mail brought disappointing news. Revise the letter. Mentally rewrite it and make it conform to the news you wish you had received. Then, in imagination, read the revised letter over and over again. This is the essence of revision and revision results in repeal.

The one requisite is to arouse your attention in a way and to such intensity that you become wholly absorbed in the revised action. You will experience an expansion and refinement of the senses by this imaginative exercise and eventually achieve vision. But always remember that the ultimate purpose of this exercise is to create in you "the Spirit of Jesus" which is continual forgiveness of sin.

Revision is of greatest importance when the motive is to change oneself, when there is a sincere desire to be something different, when the longing is to awaken the ideal active spirit of forgiveness. Without imagination man remains a being of sin. Man either goes forward to imagination or remains imprisoned in his senses. To go forward to imagination is to forgive. Forgiveness is the life of the imagination. The art of living is the art of forgiving. Forgiveness is, in fact, experiencing in imagination the revised version of the day, experiencing in imagination what you wish you had experienced in the flesh. Every time one really forgives; that is, every time one relives the event as it should have been lived, one is born again.

"Father forgive them" is not the plea that comes once a year but the opportunity that comes every day. The idea of forgiving is a daily possibility, and, if it is sincerely done, it will lift man to higher and higher levels of being. He will experience a daily Easter and

Easter is the idea of rising transformed. And that should be almost a continuous process.

Freedom and forgiveness are indissolubly linked. Not to forgive is to be at war with ourselves for we are freed according to our capacity to forgive.

> *"Forgive, and you shall be forgiven."*
>
> LUKE 6:37

Forgive, not merely from a sense of duty or service, forgive because you want to.

> *"Thy ways are ways of pleasantness and all thy paths are peace."*
>
> PROVERBS 3:17

You must take pleasure in revision. You can forgive others effectively only when you have a sincere desire to identify them with their ideal. Duty has no momentum. Forgiveness is a matter of deliberately withdrawing attention from the unrevised day and giving it full strength and joyously to the revised day. If a man begins to revise even a little of the vexations and troubles of the day, then he begins to work practically on himself. Every revision is a victory over himself and therefore a victory over his enemy.

> *"A man's foes are those of his own household."*
>
> MATTHEW 10:36

and his household is his state of mind. He changes his future as he revises his day.

When man practices the art of forgiveness, of revision, however factual the scene on which sight then rests, he revises it with his imagination and gazes on one never before witnessed. The magnitude of the change which any act of revision involves makes such change appear wholly improbable to the realist—the unimaginative man; but the radical changes in the fortunes of the Prodigal were all produced by a 'change of heart.'

The battle man fights is fought out *in his own imagination*. The man who does not revise the day has lost the vision of that life, into the likeness of which, it is the true labour of the 'Spirit of Jesus' to transform this life.

> *"All things whatsoever ye would that men should do to*
> *you, even so do ye to them: for this is the law."*
>
> MATTHEW 7:12

Here is the way an artist friend forgave herself and was set free from pain, annoyance and unfriendliness. Knowing that nothing but forgetfulness and forgiveness will bring us to new values, she cast herself upon her imagination and escaped from the prison of her senses. She writes:

"Thursday I taught all day in the art school. Only one small thing marred the day. Coming into my afternoon classroom I discovered the janitor had left all the chairs on top of the desks after cleaning the floor. As I lifted a chair down it slipped from my grasp and struck me a sharp blow on the instep of my right foot. I immediately examined my thoughts and found that I had criticized the man for not doing his job properly. Since he had lost his helper I realized he probably felt he had done more than enough and it was an unwanted gift that had bounced and hit me on the foot. Looking down at my foot I saw both my skin and nylons were intact so forgot the whole thing. "That night, after I had been working intensely for about three hours on a drawing, I decided to make myself a cup of coffee. To my utter amazement I couldn't manage my right foot at all and it was giving out great bumps of pain. I hopped over to a chair and took off my slipper to look at it. The entire foot was a strange purplish pink, swollen out of shape and red hot. I tried walking on it and found that it just flapped. I had no control over it whatsoever. It looked like one of two things: either I had cracked a bone when I dropped the chair on it or something could be dislocated.

"'No use speculating what it is. Better get rid of it right away.' So I became quiet all ready to melt myself into light. To my complete bewilderment my imagination refused to cooperate. It just said 'No.' This sort of thing often happens when I am painting. I just started to argue 'Why not?' It just kept saying 'No.' Finally I gave up and said 'You know I am in pain. I am trying hard not to be frightened, but you are the boss. What do you want to do?' The answer: 'Go to bed and review the day's events.' So I said 'All right. But let me tell you if my foot isn't perfect by tomorrow morning you have only yourself to blame.'

"After arranging the bed clothes so they didn't touch my foot I started to review the day. It was slow going as I had difficulty keeping my attention away from my foot. I went through the whole day, saw nothing to add to the chair incident. But when I reached the early evening I found myself coming face to face with a man who for the past year has made a point of not speaking. The first time this happened I thought he had grown deaf. I had known him since school days, but we had never done more than say 'hello' and comment on the weather. Mutual friends assured me I had done nothing, that he had said he never liked me and finally decided it was not worthwhile speaking. I had said 'Hi!' He hadn't answered. I found that I thought 'Poor guy—what a horrid state to be in. I shall do something about this ridiculous state of affairs,' So, in my imagination, I stopped right there and re-did the scene. I said 'Hi!' He answered 'Hi!' and smiled. I now thought 'Good old Ed.' I ran the scene over a couple of times and went on to the next incident and finished up the day.

"'Now what—do we do my foot or the concert?' I had been melting and wrapping up a wonderful present of courage and success for a friend who was to make her debut the following day and I had been looking forward to giving it to her tonight. My imagination sounded a little bit solemn as it said 'Let us do the concert. It will be more fun.' 'But first couldn't we just take my perfectly good imagination foot out of this physical one before we start?' I pleaded. 'By all means.'

"That done, I had a lovely time at the concert and my friend got a tremendous ovation.

"By now I was very, very sleepy and fell asleep doing my project. The next morning, as I was putting on my slipper, I suddenly had a quick memory picture of withdrawing a discolored and swollen foot from the same slipper. I took my foot out and looked at it. It was perfectly normal in every respect. There was a tiny pink spot on the instep where I remembered I had hit it with the chair. 'What a vivid dream that was!' I thought and dressed. While waiting for my coffee I wandered over to my drafting table and saw that all my brushes were lying helter-skelter and unwashed. 'Whatever possessed you to leave your brushes like that?' 'Don't you remember? It was because of your foot.' So it hadn't been a dream after all but a beautiful healing."

She had won by the art of revision what she would never have won by force.

> *"In Heaven the only Art of Living Is Forgetting &*
> *Forgiving Especially to the Female."*
>
> BLAKE

We should take our life, not as it appears to be, but from the vision of this artist, from the vision of the world made perfect that is buried under all minds—buried and waiting for us to revise the day.

> *"We are led to believe a lie when we see with, not*
> *through the eye."*

BLAKE

A revision of the day, and what she held to be so stubbornly real was no longer so to her and, like a dream, had quietly faded away.

You can revise the day to please yourself and by experiencing in imagination the revised speech and actions not only modify the trend of your life story but turn all its discords into harmonies. The one who discovers the secret of revision cannot do otherwise than let himself be guided by love. Your effectiveness will increase with practice. Revision is the way by which right can find its appropriate might. "Resist not evil" for all passionate conflicts result in an interchange of characteristics.

> *"To him that knoweth to do good, and doeth it not, to*
> *him it is sin."*

JAMES 4:17

To know the truth you must live the truth and to live the truth your inner actions must match the actions of your fulfilled desire. Expectancy and desire must become one. Your outer world is only actualized inner movement. Through ignorance of the law of revision those who take to warfare are perpetually defeated.

Only concepts that idealize depict the truth.

Your ideal of man is his truest self. It is because I firmly believe that whatever is most profoundly imaginative is, in reality, most directly practical that I ask you to live imaginatively and to think into and to personally appropriate the transcendent saying "Christ in you, the hope of glory."

Don't blame; only resolve. It is not man and the earth at their loveliest, but you practicing the art of revision make paradise. The evidence of this truth can lie only in your own experience of it. Try revising the day. It is to the pruning shears of revision that we owe our prime fruit.

5

THE COIN OF HEAVEN

"Does a firm persuasion that a thing is so, make it so?" And the prophet replied "All poets believe that it does. And in ages of imagination this firm persuasion removed mountains: but many are not capable of a firm persuasion of anything."

WILLIAM BLAKE,
"MARRIAGE OF HEAVEN AND HELL."

"Let every man be fully persuaded in his own mind."
ROMANS 14:5

Persuasion is an inner effort of intense attention. To listen attentively as though you heard is to evoke, to activate. By listening you can hear what you want to hear and persuade those beyond the range of the outer ear. Speak it inwardly in your imagination only. Make your inner conversation match your fulfilled desire. What you desire to hear without, you must hear within. Embrace the without within and become one who hears only that which implies the fulfillment of his desire, and all the external happenings in the world will become a bridge leading to the objective realization of your desire.

Your inner speech is perpetually written all around you in happenings. Learn to relate these happenings to your inner speech and you will become self-taught. By inner speech is meant those mental conversations which you carry on with yourself. They may be inaudible when you are awake because of the noise and distractions of the outer world of becoming, but they are quite audible in deep meditation and dream. But whether they be audible or inaudible, you are their author and fashion your world in their likeness.

> "There is a God in heaven," and heaven is within you, "that revealeth secrets, and maketh known to the king Nebuchadnezzar what shall be in the latter days. Thy dream, and the visions of thy head upon thy bed, are these."

> DANIEL 2:28

Inner speech from premises of fulfilled desire is the way to create an intelligible world for yourself. Observe your inner speech for it is the cause of future action. Inner speech reveals the state of consciousness from which you view the world. Make your inner speech match your fulfilled desire, for your inner speech is manifested all around you in happenings.

> "If any man offend not in word, the same is a perfect man and able also to bridle the whole body. Behold we put bits in the horses' mouths, that they may obey us;

and we turn about their whole body. Behold also the
ships, which though they be so great, and are driven
by fierce winds, yet are they turned about with a very
small helm, whithersoever the governor listeth. Even so
the tongue is a little member, and boasteth great things.
Behold, how great a matter a little fire kindleth."

JAMES 3:2-5

The whole manifested world goes to show us what use we have made of the Word—Inner Speech. An uncritical observation of our inner talking will reveal to us the ideas from which we view the world. Inner talking mirrors our imagination and our imagination mirrors the state with which it is fused. If the state with which we are fused is the cause of the phenomenon of our life, then we are relieved of the burden of wondering what to do, for we have no alternative but to identify ourselves with our aim; and inasmuch as the state with which we are identified mirrors itself in our inner speech, then to change the state with which we are fused, we must first change our inner talking. It is our inner conversations which make tomorrow's facts.

"Put off the former conversation, the old man, which
is corrupt . . . and be renewed in the spirit of your
mind . . . put on the new man, which is created in
righteousness."

EPHESIANS 4:22-24

"Our minds, like our stomachs, are whetted by change of food."

QUINTILLIAN

Stop all of the old mechanical negative inner talking and start a new positive and constructive inner speech from premises of fulfilled desire. Inner talking is the beginning, the sowing of the seeds of future action. To determine the action, you must consciously initiate and control your inner talking. Construct a sentence which implies the fulfillment of your aim, such as "I have a large steady dependable income, consistent with integrity and mutual benefit," or "I am happily married." "I am wanted." "I am contributing to the good of the world," and repeat such a sentence over and over until you are inwardly affected by it. Our inner speech represents in various ways the world we live in.

"In the beginning was the Word,"

JOHN 1:1

"That which ye sow ye reap. See yonder fields! The sesamum was sesamum, the corn was corn. The Silence and the Darkness Knew! So is a man's fate born."

THE LIGHT OF ASIA

Ends run true to origins.

*"Those that go searching for love only make manifest
their own lovelessness. And the loveless never find
love, only the loving find love, and they never have to
seek for it."*

D. H. LAWRENCE

Man attracts what he *is.* The art of life is to sustain the feeling of the wish fulfilled and let things come to you, not to go after them or think they flee away.

Observe your inner talking and remember your aim. Do they match? Does your inner talking match what you would say audibly had you achieved your goal? The individual's inner speech and actions attract the conditions of his life. Through uncritical self-observation of your inner talking you find where you are in the inner world, and where you are in the inner world is what you are in the outer world. You put on the new man whenever ideals and inner speech match. In this way alone can the new man be born.

Inner talking matures in the dark. From the dark it issues into the light. The right inner speech is the speech that would be yours were you to realize your ideal. In other words, it is the speech of fulfilled desire.

"I am that.

*"There are two gifts which God has bestowed upon
man alone, and on no other mortal creature. These
two are mind and speech; and the gift of mind and*

speech is equivalent to that of immortality. If a man
uses these two gifts rightly, he will differ in nothing from
the immortals . . . and when he quits the body, mind
and speech will be his guides, and by them he will be
brought into the troop of the gods and the souls that
have attained to bliss."

WALTER SCOTT'S TRANSLATION
"HERMETICA," VOL. 1, P. 231

The circumstances and conditions of life are out-pictured inner talking, solidified sound. Inner speech calls events into existence. In every event is the creative sound that is its life and being. All that a man believes and consents to as true reveals itself in his inner speech. It is his Word, his life.

Try to notice what you are saying in yourself at this moment, to what thoughts and feelings you are consenting. They will be perfectly woven into your tapestry of life. To change your life you must change your inner talking for "life," said Hermes, "is the union of Word and Mind." When imagination matches your inner speech to fulfilled desire there will then be a straight path in yourself from within out, and the without will instantly reflect the within for you, and you will know reality is only actualized inner talking.

"Receive with meekness the inborn Word which is able
to save your souls."

JAMES 1:21

Every stage of man's progress is made by the conscious exercise of his imagination matching his inner speech to his fulfilled desire. Because man does not perfectly match them the results are uncertain while they might be perfectly certain. Persistent assumption of the wish fulfilled is the means of fulfilling the intention. As we control our inner talking, matching it to our fulfilled desires, we can lay aside all other processes. Then we simply act by clear imagination and intention. We imagine the wish fulfilled and carry on mental conversations from that premise.

Through controlled inner talking from premises of fulfilled desire seeming miracles are performed. The future becomes the present and reveals itself in our inner speech. To be held by the inner speech of fulfilled desire is to be safely anchored in life. Our lives may seem to be broken by events but they are never broken so long as we retain the inner speech of fulfilled desire. All happiness depends on the active voluntary use of imagination to construct and inwardly affirm that we are what we want to be. We match ourselves to our ideals by constantly remembering our aim and identifying ourselves with it. We fuse with our aims by frequently occupying the feeling of our wish fulfilled. It is the frequency, the habitual occupancy, that is the secret of success. The oftener we do it, the more natural it is. Fancy assembles. Continuous imagination fuses.

It is possible to resolve every situation by the proper use of imagination. Our task is to get the right sentence, the one which implies that our desire is realized and fire the imagination with it. All this is intimately connected with the mystery of "the still small voice."

Inner talking reveals the activities of imagination, activities which are the causes of the circumstances of life. As a rule man is totally unaware of his inner talking and therefore sees himself not as the cause but the victim of circumstance. To consciously create circumstance man must consciously direct his inner speech, matching "the still small voice" to his fulfilled desires.

> *"He calls things not seen as though they were."*
>
> ROMANS 4:17

Right inner speech is essential. It is the greatest of the arts. It is the way out of limitation into freedom. Ignorance of this art has made the world a battlefield and penitentiary where blood and sweat alone are expected, when it should be a place of marvelling and wondering. Right inner talking is the first step to becoming what you want to be.

> *"Speech is an image of mind, and mind is an image of God."*
>
> HERMETICA, VOL. 1. P. 231

On the morning of April 12, 1953, my wife was awakened by the sound of a great voice of authority speaking within her and saying, "You must stop spending your thoughts, time and money. Everything in life must be an investment."

To spend is to waste, to squander, to lay out without return. To invest is to lay out for a purpose from which a profit is expected.

This revelation of my wife is about the importance of the moment. It is about the transformation of the moment. What we desire does not lie in the future but in ourselves at this very moment. At any moment in our lives we are faced with an infinite choice: 'what we are and what we want to be.' And what we want to be is already existent, but to realize it we must match our inner speech and actions to it.

> *"If two of you shall agree on earth as touching anything*
> *that they shall ask, it shall be done for them of my*
> *Father which is in heaven."*
>
> MATTHEW 18:19

It is only what is done *now* that counts. The present moment does not recede into the past. It advances into the future to confront us, spent or invested. Thought is the coin of heaven. Money is its earthly symbol. Every moment must be invested and our inner talking reveals whether we are spending or investing. Be more interested in what you are inwardly 'saying now' than what you have 'said' by choosing wisely what you think and what you feel *now*.

Any time we feel misunderstood, misused, neglected, suspicious, afraid, we are spending our thoughts and wasting our time. Whenever we assume the feeling of being what we want to be, we are investing. We cannot abandon the moment to negative inner talking and expect to retain command of life. Before us goes the results of all that seemingly is behind. Not gone is the last moment—but oncoming.

"My word shall not return unto me void, but it shall accomplish that which I please, and it shall prosper in the thing whereto I sent it."

ISAIAH 55:11

The circumstances of life are the muffled utterances of the inner talking that made them—the word made visible.

"The Word," said Hermes, "is Son, and the Mind is Father of the Word. They are not separate one from the other; for life is the union of Word and Mind."

"He willed us forth from Himself by the Word of truth."

JAMES 1:18

Let us

"be imitators of God as dear children"

EPHESIANS 5:1

and use our inner speech wisely to mould an outer world in harmony with our ideal.

"The Lord spake by me, and his Word was in my tongue."

2 SAMUEL 23:2

The mouth of God is the mind of man. Feed God only the best.

*"Whatsoever things are of good report . . . think on
these things."*

PHILIPPIANS 4:8

The present moment is always precisely right for an investment, to inwardly speak the right word.

*"The word is very near to you, in your mouth, and in
your heart, that you may do it. See, I have set before
you this day life and good, death and evil, blessings and
cursings, choose life."*

DEUTERONOMY 30:14-15

You choose life and good and blessings by *being* that which you
choose. Like is known to like alone. Make your inner speech bless
and give good reports. Man's ignorance of the future is the result
of his ignorance of his inner talking. His inner talking mirrors his
imagination and his imagination is a government in which the
opposition never comes into power.

If the reader ask "What if the inner speech remains subjective and is unable to find an object for its love?" the answer is: it
will not remain subjective, for the very simple reason that inner
speech is always objectifying itself. What frustrates and festers and
becomes the disease that afflicts humanity is man's ignorance of
the art of matching inner words to fulfilled desire. Inner speech
mirrors imagination and imagination is Christ.

Alter your inner speech, and your perceptual world changes. Whenever inner speech and desire are in conflict inner speech invariably wins. Because inner speech objectifies itself, it is easy to see that if it matches desire, desire will be objectively realized. Were this not so I would say with Blake

> "Sooner murder an infant in its cradle than nurse unacted desires."

But I know from experience

> "The tongue . . . setteth on fire the course of nature."
>
> JAMES 3:6

6

IT IS WITHIN

"... Rivers, Mountains, Cities, Villages, All are
Human, & when you enter into their Bosoms
you walk In Heavens & Earths, as in your
own Bosom you bear your Heaven And Earth
& all you behold; tho' it appears Without,
it is Within, In your Imagination, of which
this World of Mortality is but a Shadow."
BLAKE: "JERUSALEM" P. 71, LINES 15-9

The inner world was as real to Blake as the outer land of waking
life. He looked upon his dreams and visions as the realities of the
forms of nature. Blake reduced everything to the bed-rock of his
own consciousness.

"The Kingdom of Heaven is within you."

LUKE 17:21

The Real Man, the Imaginative Man, has invested the outer
world with all of its properties. The apparent reality of the outer

world which is so hard to dissolve is only proof of the absolute reality of the inner world of his own imagination.

> *"No man can come to me, except the Father which*
> *hath sent me draw him: . . . I and my Father are one."*
>
> JOHN 6:44, JOHN 10:30

The world which is described from observation is a manifestation of the mental activity of the observer. When man discovers that his world is his own mental activity made visible, that no man can come unto him except he draws him, and that there is no one to change but himself, his own imaginative self, his first impulse is to reshape the world in the image of his ideal. But his ideal is not so easily incarnated. In that moment when he ceases to conform to external discipline he must impose upon himself a far more rigorous discipline, the self-discipline upon which the realization of his ideal depends.

Imagination is not entirely untrammelled and free to move at will without any rules to constrain it. In fact, the contrary is true. Imagination travels according to habit. Imagination has choice, but it chooses according to habit. Awake or asleep, man's imagination is constrained to follow certain definite patterns. It is this benumbing influence of habit that man must change; if he does not, his dreams will fade under the paralysis of custom.

Imagination, which is Christ in man, is not subject to the necessity to produce only that which is perfect and good. It exercises its absolute freedom from necessity by endowing the outer physical self with free will to choose to follow good or evil, order or disorder.

> *"Choose this day whom ye will serve."*
>
> JOSHUA 24:15

But after the choice is made and accepted so that it forms the individual's habitual consciousness, then imagination manifests its infinite power and wisdom by moulding the outer sensuous world of becoming in the image of the habitual inner speech and actions of the individual.

To realize his ideal man must first change the pattern which his imagination has followed. Habitual thought is indicative of character. The way to change the outer world is to make the inner speech and action match the outer speech and action of fulfilled desire.

Our ideals are waiting to be incarnated but unless we ourselves match our inner speech and action to the speech and action of fulfilled desire, they are incapable of birth. Inner speech and action are the channels of God's action. He cannot respond to our prayer unless these paths are offered. The outer behavior of man is mechanical. It is subject to the compulsion applied to it by the behavior of the inner self, and old habits of the inner self hang on till replaced by new ones. It is a peculiar property of the second or inner man that he gives to the outer self something similar to his own reality of being. Any change in the behavior of the inner self will result in corresponding outer changes.

The mystic calls a change of consciousness 'death.' By death he means, not the destruction of imagination and the state with which it was fused, but the dissolution of their union. Fusion is union rather than oneness. Thus the conditions to which that union gave being vanish. "I die daily," said Paul to the Corinthians. Blake said to his friend Crabbe Robinson:

> "There is nothing like death. Death is the best thing
> that can happen in life; but most people die so late and
> take such an unmerciful time in dying. God knows,
> their neighbors never see them rise from the dead."

To the outer man of sense, who knows nothing of the inner man of Being, this is sheer nonsense. But Blake made the above quite clear when he wrote in the year before he died:

> "William Blake—one who is very much delighted with
> being in good company. Born 28 November 1757 in
> London and has died several times since."

When man has the sense of Christ *as his imagination,* he sees why Christ must die and rise again from the dead to save man— why he must detach his imagination from his present state and match it to a higher concept of himself if he would rise above his present limitations and thereby save himself.

Here is a lovely story of a mystical death which was witnessed by a 'neighbor.' "Last week," writes the one 'who rose from the dead,' "a friend offered me her home in the mountains for the Christmas holidays as she thought she might go east. She said that she would let me know this week. We had a very pleasant conversation and I mentioned you and your teaching in connection with a discussion of Dunne's 'Experiment With Time' which she had been reading.

"Her letter arrived Monday. As I picked it up I had a sudden sense of depression. However, when I read it she said I could have the house and told me where to get the keys. Instead of being cheerful I grew still more depressed, so much so I decided there must have been something between the lines which I was getting intuitively. I unfolded the letter and read the first page through and as I turned to the second page, I noticed she had written a postscript on the back of the first sheet. It consisted of an extremely blunt and heavy-handed description of an unlovely trait in my character which I had struggled for years to overcome and for the past two years I thought I had succeeded. Yet here it was again, described with clinical exactitude.

"I was stunned and desolated. I thought to myself, 'What is this letter trying to tell me? In the first place she invited me to use her house as I have been seeing myself in some lovely home during the holidays. In the second place, nothing comes to me except I draw it. And thirdly I have been hearing *nothing* but good news. So the obvious conclusion is that something in me corresponds to this letter and no matter what it looks like it is good news.'

"I reread the letter and as I did so I asked 'What is there here for me to see?' And then I saw. It started out 'After our conversation of last week I feel I can tell you' and the rest of the page was as studded with 'weres' and 'wases' as currants in a seed cake. A great feeling of elation swept over me. It was *all* in the past. The thing I had labored so long to correct was *done*. I suddenly realized that my friend was a witness to my resurrection. I whirled around the studio chanting 'It's all in the past! It is done. Thank you, it is done!' I gathered all my gratitude up in a big ball of light and shot it straight to you and if you saw a flash of lightning Monday evening shortly after six your time, that was it.

"Now, instead of writing a polite letter because it is the correct thing to do, I can write giving sincere thanks for her frankness and thanking her for the loan of her house. Thank you so much for your teaching which has made my beloved imagination truly my Saviour."

And now, if any man shall say unto her

"*Lo, here is Christ, or there,*"

she will believe it not, for she knows that the Kingdom of God is within her and that she herself must assume full responsibility for the incarnation of her ideal and that nothing but death and resurrection will bring her to it. She has found her Saviour, her beloved Imagination, forever expanding in the bosom of God.

There is only one reality, and that is Christ—Human Imagination, the inheritance and final achievement of the whole of Humanity

"That we . . . speaking the truth in love, may grow up into him in all things, which is the head, even Christ."

EPHESIANS 4:15

7

CREATION IS FINISHED

> *"I am the beginning and the end, there is*
> *nothing to come that has not been, and is."*
> **ECCLESIASTES 3:15 ERV**

Blake saw all possible human situations as "already-made" *states*. He saw every aspect, every plot and drama as already worked out as 'mere possibilities' as long as we are not in them, but as overpowering realities when we are in them. He described these states as "Sculptures of Los's Halls."

> *"Distinguish therefore states from Individuals in those*
> *States. States change but Individual Identities never*
> *change nor cease ... The Imagination is not a State,"*

Said Blake,

> *"It is the Human Existence itself. Affection or Love*
> *becomes a State when divided from Imagination."*

Just how important this is to remember is almost impossible to say, but the moment the individual realizes this for the first time is the most momentous in his life, and to be encouraged to feel this is the highest form of encouragement it is possible to give. This truth is common to all men, but the consciousness of it, and much more, the self-consciousness of it, is another matter.

The day I realized this great truth—that everything in my world is a manifestation of the mental activity which goes on within me, and that the conditions and circumstances of my life only reflect the state of consciousness with which I am fused—is the most momentous in my life. But the experience that brought me to this certainty is so remote from ordinary existence I have long hesitated to tell it, for my reason refused to admit the conclusions to which the experience impelled me. Nevertheless, this experience revealed to me that I am supreme within the circle of my own state of consciousness and that it is the state with which I am identified that determines what I experience. Therefore it should be shared with all, for to know this is to become free from the world's greatest tyranny, the belief in a second cause.

> *"Blessed are the pure in heart: for they shall see God."*
> MATTHEW 5:8

Blessed are they whose imagination has been so purged of the beliefs in second causes they know that imagination is all and all is imagination.

One day I quietly slipped from my apartment in New York City into some remote yesteryear's countryside. As I entered the dining room of a large inn I became fully conscious. I knew that my physical body was immobilized on my bed back in New York City. Yet here I was as awake and as conscious as I have ever been. I intuitively knew that if I could stop the activity of my mind everything before me would freeze. No sooner was the thought born than the urge to try it possessed me. I felt my head tighten, then thicken to a stillness. My attention concentrated into a crystal-clear focus and the waitress walking, walked not. And I looked through the window and the leaves falling, fell not. And the family of four eating, ate not. And they lifting the food, lifted it not. Then my attention relaxed, the tightness eased, and of a sudden all moved onward in their course. The leaves fell, the waitress walked and the family ate. Then I understood Blake's vision of the "Sculptures of Los's Halls."

> *"I sent you to reap that whereon ye bestowed no labor."*
>
> JOHN 4:35

Creation is finished.

> *"I am the beginning and the end, there is nothing to*
> *come that has not been, and is."*
>
> ECCLESIASTES 3:15, ERV

The world of creation is finished and its original is within us. We saw it before we set forth, and have since been trying to remember it and to activate sections of it. There are infinite views of it. Our task is to get the right view and by determined direction of our attention make it pass in procession before the inner eye. If we assemble the right sequence and experience it in imagination until it has the tone of reality, then we consciously create circumstances. This inner procession is the activity of imagination that must be consciously directed. We, by a series of mental transformations, become aware of increasing portions of that which already is, and by matching our own mental activity to that portion of creation which we desire to experience we activate it, resurrect it and give it life.

This experience of mine not only shows the world as a manifestation of the mental activity of the individual observer, but it also reveals our course of time as jumps of attention between eternal moments. An infinite abyss separates any two moments of ours. We by the movements of our attention give life to the "Sculptures of Los's Halls."

Think of the world as containing an infinite number of states of consciousness from which it could be viewed. Think of these states as rooms or mansions in the House of God, and like the rooms of any house they are fixed relative to one another. But think of yourself, the Real Self, the Imaginative You, as the living, moving occupant of God's House. Each room contains some of Los's Sculptures, with infinite plots and dramas and situations already worked out but not activated. They are activated as soon as Human Imagination enters and fuses with them. Each represents certain mental and emotional activities. To enter a state man must consent to the ideas and feelings which it represents. These states represent an infinite number of possible mental transformations which man can experience. To move into another state or mansion necessitates a change of beliefs. All that you could ever desire is already present and only waits to be matched by your beliefs. But it must be matched, for that is the necessary condition by which alone it can be activated and objectified. Matching the beliefs of a state is the seeking that finds, the knocking to which is opened, the asking that receives. Go in and possess the land.

The moment man matches the beliefs of any state he fuses with it and this union results in the activation and projection of its plots, plans, dramas and situations. It becomes the individual's home from which he views the world. It is his workshop, and, if he is observant, he will see outer reality shaping itself upon the model of his imagination.

It is for this purpose of training us in image-making that we were made subject to the limitations of the senses and clothed in bodies of flesh. It is the awakening of the imagination, the return-ing of His Son, that our Father waits for.

> "The creature was made subject to vanity not willingly
> but by reason of Him who subjected it."
>
> ROMANS 8:20

But the victory of the Son, the return of the prodigal, assures us that

> "the creature shall be delivered from the bondage of
> corruption into the glorious liberty of the Sons of God."
>
> ROMANS 8:21

We were subjected to this biological experience because no one can know of imagination who has not been subjected to the vanities and limitations of the flesh, who has not taken his share of Sonship and gone prodigal, who has not experimented and tasted this cup of experience; and confusion will continue until man awakes and a fundamentally imaginative view of life has been reestablished and acknowledged as basic.

> *"I should preach the unsearchable riches of Christ and make all men see what is the fellowship of the mystery, which from the beginning of the world has been hid in God, who created all things by Jesus Christ."*
>
> EPHESIANS 3:9

Bear in mind that Christ in you is your imagination.

As the appearance of our world is determined by the particular state with which we are fused, so may we determine our fate as individuals by fusing our imaginations with ideals we seek to realize. On the distinction between our states of consciousness depends the distinction between the circumstances and conditions of our lives. Man who is free in his choice of state often cries out to be saved from the state of his choice.

> *"And ye shall cry out in that day because of your king which ye shall have chosen you; and the Lord will not hear you in that day. Nevertheless the people refused to*

obey the voice of Samuel; and they said, Nay; but we
will have a king over us."

1 SAMUEL 8:18, 19

Choose wisely the state that you will serve. All states are lifeless until imagination fuses with them.

"All things when they are admitted are made manifest by
the light: for everything that is made manifest is light."

EPHESIANS 5:13

and

"Ye are the light of the world,"

MATTHEW 5:14

by which those ideas to which you have consented are made manifest.

Hold fast to your ideal. Nothing can take it from you but your imagination. Don't think *of* your ideal, think *from* it. It is only the ideals *from* which you think that are ever realized.

"Man lives not by bread alone, but by every word that
proceeds out of the mouth of God."

MATTHEW 4:4

and 'the mouth of God' is the mind of man.

Become a drinker and an eater of the ideals you wish to realize. Have a set definite aim or your mind will wander and wandering it eats every negative suggestion. If you live right mentally everything else will be right. By a change of mental diet you can alter the course of observed events. But unless there is a change of mental diet your personal history remains the same. You illuminate or darken your life by the ideas to which you consent. Nothing is more important to you than the ideas on which you feed. And you feed on the ideas *from* which you think. If you find the world unchanged it is a sure sign that you are wanting in fidelity to the new mental diet which you neglect in order to condemn your environment. You are in need of a new and sustained attitude. You can be anything you please if you will make the conception habitual, for any idea which excludes all others from the field of attention discharges in action. The ideas and moods to which you constantly return define the state with which you are fused. Therefore train yourself to occupy more frequently the feeling of your wish fulfilled. This is creative magic. It is the way to work toward fusion with the desired state.

If you would assume the feeling of your wish fulfilled more frequently you would be master of your fate, but unfortunately you shut out your assumption for all but the occasional hour. Practice making real to yourself the feeling of the wish fulfilled. After you have assumed the feeling of the wish fulfilled, do not close the experience as you would a book, but carry it around like a fragrant odor. Instead of being completely forgotten let it remain in the atmosphere communicating its influence automatically to your actions and reactions. A mood, often repeated, gains a momentum that is hard to break or check. So be careful of the feelings you entertain. Habitual moods reveal the state with which you are fused.

It is always possible to pass from thinking *of* the end you desire to realize, to thinking *from* the end. But the crucial matter is thinking *from* the end, for thinking *from* means unification or fusion with the idea: whereas in thinking *of* the end there is always subject and object—the thinking individual and the thing thought. You must imagine yourself into the state of your wish fulfilled, in your love for that state, and in so doing live and think *from* it and no more *of* it. You pass from thinking *of* to thinking *from* by centering your imagination in the feeling of the wish fulfilled.

8

THE APPLE
OF GOD'S EYE

"What think ye of the Christ?
Whose Son is He?"

MATTHEW 22:42

When this question is asked of you, let your answer be, "Christ is my imagination," and, though I

"See not yet all things put under him,"

HEBREWS 2:8

yet I know that I am Mary from whom sooner or later He shall be born, and eventually

"Do all things through Christ."

The birth of Christ is the awakening of the inner or Second man. It is becoming conscious of the mental activity within oneself, which activity continues whether we are conscious of it or not.

The birth of Christ does not bring any person from a distance, or make anything to be that was not there before. It is the unveiling of the Son of God in man. The Lord "cometh in clouds" is the prophet's description of the pulsating rings of golden liquid light on the head of him in whom He awakes. The coming is from within and not from without, as Christ is *in* us.

This great mystery

"God was manifest in the flesh"

begins with Advent, and it is appropriate that the cleansing of the Temple

"Which temple ye are,"

1 CORINTHIANS 3:17

stands in the forefront of the Christian mysteries.

"The Kingdom of Heaven is within you."

LUKE 17:21

Advent is unveiling the mystery of your being. If you will practice the art of revision by a life lived according to the wise, imaginative use of your inner speech and inner actions, in confidence that by the conscious use of "the power that worketh in us," Christ will awake in you. If you will believe it, trust it, act upon it, Christ will awake in you. This is Advent.

"Great is the mystery, God was manifest in the flesh."

1 TIMOTHY 3:16

From Advent on

"He that toucheth you toucheth the apple of God's eye."

ZECHARIAH 2:8

II

CHARIOT OF FIRE: THE IDEAS OF NEVILLE GODDARD

By Mitch Horowitz

This was my first public talk on Neville, delivered June 28, 2013, at the now-defunct arts space Observatory in Gowanus, Brooklyn. It includes the complete talk and the question-and-answer session that followed. —MH

S ome of you know my work, my book *Occult America,* and things that I've done related to that. *Occult America* is a history of supernatural religious movements in our country. A few of you who know my work are aware that I feel strongly that occult, esoteric, and metaphysical movements have touched this country very deeply. I write about these movements not only as a historian who is passionately interested in how the paranormal, occult, and supernatural have influenced our religion, our economy, our psychology, and our views of ourselves; but I also write about these things as a participant, as a kind of a believing historian. I do not view occult thought movements strictly as historical phenomena, which may reveal aspects of human nature; that's true enough, but I think that within the folds of such movements there exist actual ideas for human transformation.

I don't believe in looking into philosophies simply in order to place them in museum cases and to label them. Rather, I think we need practical philosophies that contribute to real-life transformation in the here and now. In my study of different occult and mystical systems, some of which I wrote about in *Occult America* and some of which I'm writing about in my next book *One Simple Idea,* I must tell you the most impactful, elegant, simplest, and dramatically powerful figure I have come across is Neville Goddard.

He was born to an Anglican family on the island of Barbados in 1905. It was a family of ten children, nine boys and one girl. Neville came here to New York City to study theater in 1922. He had some success and also fell into a variety of mystical and occult philosophies. Neville eventually came to feel that he had discovered the master key to existence. Up to this point in my experiments, I conclude: he may have been right.

You can determine that for yourself, because I'm going to start off this presentation by giving you his system. I am also going to provide some history: where he came from, who his teachers were, what his ideas grew out of, who he has influenced, and why he proved vastly ahead of his time. Some of the methods and ideas that Neville experimented with are being heard about today through unsensationalized discussions of developments in quantum physics and neurobiology.

I will also consider the possible identity of the hidden spiritual master named Abdullah who Neville said was his teacher in New York City. Are there spiritual masters, masters of wisdom in the world? Are there beings who can provide help to us when we sincerely desire it? Is that a real possibility or is that just fantasy? I think it's a possibility. It may have played out in his existence.

But we're really here to talk about the practical side of his philosophy. There are many interesting figures who I reference in this talk—dramatic figures whose lives spanned the globe. But we're talking about Neville *because of the usefulness of his ideas* and I want to start with that.

Mind as God

Neville believed very simply in the principle that your imagination is God, the human imagination is God, and that Scripture and all the stories from Scripture, both Old Testament and New Testament, have absolutely no basis in historical reality. The entire book is a metaphor, a blueprint for the individual's personal development. In particular, the New Testament tells the story of God symbolically, of God descending into human form, of humanity becoming asleep to its own divine essence or Christ essence, and believing itself to live within a coarse, limited world of material parameters, of then being crucified and experiencing the agony of his forgetfulness. Christ yells out in the across, "My God, my God, why hast thou forsaken me?" The individual is then resurrected into the realization of his or her divine potentiality, which is the birthright of every individual.

Neville maintained, through his reading of Scripture, his personal probing as a philosopher, and his experiments as an individual, that there is no God outside of the creative powers of the imagination; and that those who wrote Scripture never intended to communicate that there was a God outside of the individual's imagination. The creative force within us—which thinks, plans, pictures, ponders, and falls in and out of emotive states—is symbolically represented in Scripture as God.

Neville maintained that your thoughts, your mental pictures, and your emotive states create your concrete reality—and do at every moment of existence. We are oblivious and asleep to this fact. We live in these coarse shells, we suffer, we cry, we have fleeting joys, we leave these forms. We go through life in a state of slumber without ever knowing that each one of us is a physical form in which creation is experiencing itself. We eventually come to the realization through our causative minds we can experience the powers written about in symbolically in the New Testament and embodied as the story of Christ resurrected.

I want to say to you that Neville meant all of this in the most radical and literal sense. There was nothing inexact or qualified in what he said. He took a radical stand and he continually put up a challenge to his audiences: *try it.* Try it tonight and if it doesn't work, discard me, discard my philosophy, prove me a liar. He sold nothing. He published a handful of books, most of which are now public domain. He gave lectures Grateful Dead-style where he allowed everybody to tape record them and distribute them freely, which is why his talks are now all over the Internet. There's nothing to join. There's nothing to buy. There's no copyright holder. There's just this man and his ideas.

Three-Step Miracle

Neville's outlook can be reduced to a three-part formula, which is incredibly simple, but also requires commitment.

First, every creative act begins with an absolute, passionate desire. It sounds so easy, doesn't it? We walk around all day long with desires; I want this, I want that, I want money, I want relationships, I want this person to pay attention to me, I want this attainment. But look again. We often have superficial understandings of our desires and we're dishonest about our desires.

We're dishonest about our desires because we don't want to say to ourselves, in our innermost thoughts, *what we really want*. Sometimes we're repulsed by our desires, and that's the truth. We live in a society that's filled with so much personal license and freedom on the surface, of course, but we often don't want to acknowledge things to ourselves that maybe we believe aren't attractive.

I want to tell a personal story and I want to be very personal with you because I'm talking to you about a man and a philosophy that is enormously challenging and practical, if you really take it seriously. I have no right to be standing here talking to you unless I tell you about some of my own experiences. I want to tell you about one of my personal experiences as it relates to this first point: *desire*. Years ago, I knew a woman who was a psychic. A nationally known person, somebody I assume some of you have heard of, not household name maybe, but well known. I thought she had a genuine psychical gift. I thought she had something.

Yet I didn't like the way she led her life because I thought, personally, that she could be a violent person—not physically violent but emotionally; she would manipulate people around her, bully people, push people around. I didn't really like her but I did feel that she had a true gift. One night I was talking to her. We were on a parking lot somewhere having conversation, and she stopped. She said to me, "You know what you want? You want power. But your problem is that you have an overdeveloped super-ego." As soon as I heard this I wanted to push it away. And I spent years pushing it away. Years pushing it away because I thought to myself, "Well, I don't want power like you. I don't want power to push people around, to bully people, to be violent towards people. I don't want that, no." So I recoiled from what she said. But it haunted me. It haunted me. I could never get away from it.

You don't know really what haunts you until you confront something in yourself, or maybe something that a sensitive person says to you, which leaves the terrible impression that they might just may be speaking the truth. So when Neville talks about desire, he's not talking about something superficial that we keep telling ourselves day after day. He really wants you to get down into the guts of things, where you might want something that makes you very uncomfortable. There are ways we don't like to see ourselves. But Neville maintains that desire is the voice of the God within you; and to walk away from it is to walk away from the potential greatness within yourself. Desire is the language of God. Neville means this in the most literal sense.

The second step is physical immobility. This is the part where you actually do something. You enter a physically immobile state. Choose the time of day when you like to meditate, whether it's early morning, whether it's late at night. The time of day Neville chose was 3:00 p.m. He would finish lunch, settle into an easy chair, and go into a drowsy state. Now, this is very important because we think of meditation typically as a state of exquisite awareness. We don't think of meditation as drowsiness. People use these terms in different ways. Neville believed—and as I will talk about this later in this presentation—that the mind is uniquely powerful and suggestible in its drowsy state, hovering just before sleep, but not yet crossing into sleep. It is a controlled reverie. Or a cognizant dream state. Sleep researchers call this hypnagogia. You enter it twice daily: at night when you're drifting off and in the morning when you're coming to (this is sometimes called hypnopompia).

Our minds are exquisitely sensitive at such times. People who suffer from depression or grief describe their early morning hours as the most difficult time of day. The reason for that, I'm convinced, is that it is a time when our rational defenses are down. We're functioning almost entirely from emotion. We are conscious but we are also in this very subtle, fine state between sleep and wakefulness, and our rational defenses are slackened. Let me tell you something vital—and I can attest to this from personal experience. If you are trying to solve a personal problem, do not do it at 5:00 in the morning. Do not.

Your rational defenses are down when you need them most.

When you need your your intellect, whether you're solving a financial problem, whether you're going through a relationship problem, whatever it is, do not use the time of day when it is at its lowest ebb. At 5 a.m. your mind isn't fully working. Your emotions are working. It is a tough, tough time to deal with problems. But it is a very unique time to deal with desires—and for the same reason. When your rational defenses are down, your mind can go in remarkable directions.

I'm going to talk later about developments in psychical research, where there are some extraordinary findings under rigorous clinical conditions, in which people are induced into this hypnagogic state, the state between sleep and wakefulness, and the mind can evince remarkable abilities.

So, Neville said to enter this state of physical immobility. You can most easily do it just before you go to sleep at night. He didn't say do it when you wake up in the morning but I think you can extrapolate that that works, too. You can also do it when you're meditating. You can do it whenever you want. It takes only a few minutes, but go into a very relaxed bodily state or just let yourself be taken into it naturally when you go to bed at night.

And now *the third step*: form a very clear, simple mental scene that would naturally occur following the fulfilment of your desire. Keep it very simple. Run it through your head as long as it feels natural.

A woman attended one of Neville's lectures in Los Angeles and told him simply that she wanted to be married. He told her to enact the mental feeling of a wedding band on her finger. Just that. Keep it very simple. Mentally feel the weight and pressure of the ring on your finger. Maybe feel yourself spinning it around on your finger. Maybe there's something you want from an individual. Select an act that seems simple. Just a handshake, perhaps. Something that communicates that you received something—recognition, a promotion, a congratulation.

You must picture yourself *within* the scene. You must see from within the scene. Don't see yourself doing something as though you're watching it on a screen. Neville was adamant about this. He would say, "If I want to imagine myself climbing a ladder, I don't *see* myself climbing a ladder. *I climb.*" You must feel hands on the ladder. Feel your weight was you step up each rung. You are not watching the scene—you are in it.

Whatever it is, find one simple, clear, persuasive, physical action that would communicate the attainment of your goal, and think from that end, think from the end of the goal fulfilled. Run this through your mind as long as it feels natural.

Neville would always say, "When you open your eyes, you'll be back here in the coarse world that you might not want to be in, but if you persist in this, your assumption will harden into fact." You may wake up, come out of your physical immobility, and discover that the world remains exactly as it was. If you want to be in Paris and you open your eyes in New York, you may be disappointed. Keep doing it and extraordinary events will unfold to secure precisely what you have pictured in your mind. Persistence is key.

Using the Emotions

Now, I want to emphasize one aspect of Neville's philosophy, which I feel that he could have gone further in explaining, and that is the necessity of your visual scene being accompanied by the attendant emotional state. We often make the mistake in the positive-mind movement of equating thought with emotions. They are different things. I have a physical existence. I have intellectual existence. I have an emotional existence. Part of why you may feel torn apart when approaching mind causation is that all of these aspects of your existence—the physical, the mental, and the emotional— are going their own way, running on separate tracks. You may vow not to eat, and you may mean it, but the body wants to eat—and next thing you know the body is in control. You may vow not to get angry—but the emotions take over and you fly into rage. You may think, "I am going to use my intellect and not my passions"—but the passions rule your action. These three forces, body, mind, and intellect, have their own lives—and intellect is the weakest among them. Otherwise we wouldn't struggle with addictions or violent outbursts or impulsive actions. But we find that we are pieces.

This presents a challenge. Because when you enact your mental scene of fulfillment, you also must attain the emotive state that you would feel in your fulfillment. When you approach this teaching you benefit from being a kind of actor or thespian, as Neville was early in his career. Method Acting is a good exercise for enacting this method. Read Stanislavski's *An Actor Prepares*. Anybody who's been trained in Method Acting often learns to use a kind of inner monologue to get themselves into an emotional state. That's a good exercise. You must get the emotions in play.

Let's say you want a promotion at work. You could picture your boss saying to you, "Congratulations—well done!" You must try to feel the emotions that you would feel in that state. Hypnagogia can also help with this because, as noted, the rational defenses are lowered and the mind is more suggestible.

To review Neville's formula: 1) Identify an intense and sincere desire. 2) Enter a state of physical immobility, i.e., the drowsy hypnagogic state. 3) Gently run a scene through your mind that would occur if your wish was fulfilled. Let it be an emotional experience.

How It Happened

I want to tell another personal story. Neville always challenged his listeners: "Test it. Test it. What do you most desire right now? Go home this night and test it. Prove me wrong," he would say. I decided to test him and I want to give you the example. It is recent to this talk, explicit, and absolutely real.

In addition to being a writer, I'm a publisher. I'm the editor-in-chief of a division of Penguin that publishes New Age and metaphysical books. After considerable effort to locate the descendants of the author, I acquired the rights to republish a 1936 self-help book called *Wake Up and Live!* by Dorothea Brande. In this book, Brande writes that the pathology of human nature is what she called a *will to fail*. We fear failure and humiliation more than we crave success, so we constantly sabotage our plans in order to avoid the possibility of failure. We procrastinate. We make excuses. We blow important due dates or wreck professional relationships because we're more frightened of failure than we are hungry for success. But Brande further believed that if you were to *act as though it were impossible to fail*, you could bypass this self-negating pattern and achieve great things.

As mentioned, I spent a year trying to find her descendants so I could buy rights to this book, and I finally did. After this effort, I learned of an audio publisher who wanted to issue out an audio edition. I do a lot of audio narration, although I was still just getting started at this point, and I told this publisher that I was eager to narrate this book. I had recorded for this publisher before. It had been successful and I thought, naturally they'll agree. But they wouldn't get back to me. My e-mails were ignored. My phone calls were ignored. I was very frustrated. I couldn't understand why they wouldn't want me to do this book. I was obviously brimming of passion for it. I had done good work before. But I just couldn't get anywhere. I was totally stuck. I was very frustrated. Finally the publisher replied to me with a decisive, "No."

I thought to myself, "Well, not only do I want to be doing more audiobooks, but this is the kind of book that I was born to read." I went into this exercise and I formed a mental picture. I'm not going to tell you what it was. It was too personal but it was also very simple. I formed a mental picture. I reviewed it faithfully two or three times a day for about two weeks.

Out of the clear blue, without any outer intervention on my part, a rights manager called to say, "Guess what? Someone else actually just bought the rights to that book. It's not with that audio publisher anymore. There's been a change. There's a new audio publisher." I said, "Please tell that new publisher that I am dying to read this book." She got back to me. The new publisher said, "I sent Horowitz an e-mail a week ago asking him to read another audiobook and he never get back to me." I had gotten no such email. I went into my spam folder and found nothing. I went into a still deeper spam filter—and there is was. We signed a deal for me to narrate a total of three books, including *Wake Up and Live!*

I went from being ignored, to being told no, to signing a three-book narration deal. That relationship became one of the most central of my professional life. That same publisher issued this book that you are now reading. I did nothing to influence any of this in the outer world. I didn't do anything or contact anybody. I just did my visualization as Neville prescribed. It ended with the new audio publisher saying, "I contacted him a week ago. Why didn't he get back to me?"

For various reasons, this episode could be considered ordinary and I'm not oblivious to that. But I can say the following: from where I stood, and from long experience, it did not appear ordinary. "Take my challenge and put my words to the test. If the law does not work, its knowledge will not comfort you, and if it is not true, you must discard it. I hope you will be bold enough to test me." That's what Neville said over and over. You don't have to join anything. You don't have to buy anything. You can go online and listen to his lectures. Many of his books can be downloaded for free. His lectures can be downloaded for free. All he would insist is: "Put me to the test. Put me to the test."

Ecce Homo

Neville was born in 1905 on the island of Barbados, as mentioned. He was not born to a wealthy, land-holding family. He was born to an Anglican family of merchants. He was one of ten children, nine boys and a girl. The family ran a food service and catering business, which later mushroomed into a highly profitable corporation. One of the things that I found about Neville is that the life details and events he claimed in his lectures often turned out to be verifiably true.

I've done a lot of work to track down and verify some of Neville's claims. He came to New York City to study theater and dancing in 1922. He didn't have any money. He was a poor kid and knocked about. He lived in a shared apartment on the Upper West Side on West 75th Street. His large family back home was not rich but over the course of time, they became very rich. They later put him on kind of an allowance or a monthly stipend. Much later, he was able to pursue his studies into the occult, into philosophy, into mysticism, completely independently.

Goddard Industries is today a major catering business in Barbados. They not only cater parties and events, but they cater for airlines. They cater for cruise ships and industrial facilities. By the standards of the West Indies, they're a large and thriving business. Everything that was said in his lectures about his family's growth in fortune is true. His father, Joe or Joseph, founded the business. Neville talks frequently about his older brother Victor, in his lectures. I'm not going to go into all the details here because I have a more exciting example that I want to bring to you, but everything that Neville described about the rise of his family's fortune matches business records and reportage in West Indian newspapers.

Neville lived in Greenwich Village for many years. In the 1940s he was at 32 Washington Square on the west side of Washington Square Park. He spent many years happily there. Now, here was a story that interested me in his lectures and I determined to track down the truth of it. Neville was drafted into the Army on November 12, 1942, just a little less than a year into America's entry to

World War II, so it was at the height of war. Everybody was being drafted. He was a little old to be drafted. He was 37 at that time, but you could still be drafted up to age 45. He tells this story in several of his lectures.

He didn't want to be in the Army. He wanted no part of the war. He wanted to return home to Greenwich Village. At that time, he was married. He had a small daughter, Victoria or Vicky. He had a son from an earlier marriage. He wanted to go back to lecturing. He was in basic training in Louisiana. He asked his commanding officer for a discharge and the commanding officer definitively refused.

So Neville said that every night he would lay down in his cot and imagine himself back home in Greenwich Village, walking around Washington Square Park, back with his wife and family. Every night he'd go to bed in this sensation.

Night after night, he did this for several weeks. And he said that finally, out of the clear blue, the commanding officer came to him and said, "Do you still want to be discharged?" Neville said, "Yes, I do." "You're being honorably discharged," the officer told him.

As I read this, I doubted it. Why would the United States want to discharge a perfectly healthy, athletic male at the height of the America's entry into the Second World War? It made no sense. I started looking for Neville's military records to see if there were other things that would back this up. Neville claimed that he entered the military in late 1942 and then he was honorably discharged about four months later using nothing other than these mental-emotive techniques.

I found Neville's surviving military records. He was, in fact, inducted into the Army on November 12, 1942. I spoke to an Army public affairs spokesman who confirmed that Neville was honorably discharged in March 1943, which is the final record of his U.S. Army pay statement. The reason for the discharge in military records is that he had to return to a "vital civilian occupation." I said to the spokesman, "This man was a metaphysical lecturer, that is not seen as a vital civilian occupation." And he said to me, "Well, unfortunately, the rest of Mr. Goddard's records were destroyed in a fire at a military records facility 1973"—one year following Neville's death.

I know that Neville was back in New York City because *The New Yorker* magazine ran surprisingly extensive profile of him in September of 1943, which places him back on the circuit. He was depicted speaking all around town—in midtown in the Actor's Church, in Greenwich Village, and he completely resumed his career, this "vital civilian occupation" as a metaphysical lecturer. Now, I can't tell you what happened. I can only tell you that the forensics as he described them were accurate. This was one of several instances in which he describes an unlikely story, claims that he used his method as I've described it them you, and, while I can't tell you exactly what happened, I can tell you that the forensics line up.

Neville filled out an application for naturalization and citizenship on September 1, 1943. His address was 32 Washington Square at the time, his age 38 years old. Everything he described in terms of his whereabouts added up.

The Source

I want to say a quick word about where this philosophy came from. Where did Neville get these ideas? His thought was wholly original but everyone has antecedents of some kind. Neville was part of a movement that I call "the positive-thinking movement." Positive-mind metaphysics was a very American philosophy, and it was very much a homegrown philosophy, but, at the same time, every thought that's ever been thought has been encountered by sensitive people in the search extending back to the mythical Hermes, who ancient people in West and Near East considered the progenitor of all ideas and all intellect.

Hermetic philosophy was a Greek-Egyptian philosophy that was written about and set down in the Greek language in the city of Alexandria a few decades following the death of Christ. Neville quotes from one of the Hermetic books in the lecture "Inner Conversations." A central Hermetic theme is that through proper preparation, diet, meditation, and prayer, the individual can be permeated by divine forces. This was a key tenet of Hermeticism. This outlook was reborn during the Renaissance when scholars and translators came to venerate the figure of Hermes Trismegistus, or thrice-greatest Hermes, a Greek term of veneration of Egypt's god of intellect Thoth. Hermes Trismegistus, a mythical man-god, was considered a great figure of antiquity by Renaissance thinkers, of a vintage as old as Moses or Abraham or older still.

Renaissance translators initially believed that the Hermetic literature—tracts that were signed by Hermes Trismegistus, whose name was adopted by Greek-Egyptian scribes—extended back to primeval antiquity. Hermetic writings were considered the source of earliest wisdom. This literature was later correctly dated to late antiquity. After the re-dating, Hermetic ideas eventually fell out of vogue. Some of the intellectual lights of the Renaissance had placed great hopes that the writings attributed to Hermes Trismegistus possessed great antiquity. And when those hopes of antiquity were and these writings were accurately dated to late antiquity, the readjustment of the timeline, I think tragically for Western civilization, convinced many people that the whole project of the Hermetic literature was somehow compromised. For that reason there are, to this day, relatively few quality translations of the Hermetic literature. The dating issue assumed too great a proportion in people's minds. The fact is, all ancient literature, just like all religions, are built from earlier ideas, and I believe the Hermetic philosophy was a retention of much older oral philosophy. Most scholars today agree with that.

In any case, the Hermetic ideas faded. Including the core principle that the human form could be permeated by something higher and could itself attain a kind of creative and clairvoyant power. These ideas that were so arousing, that created such hope and intrigue during Renaissance, got pushed to the margins. But they eventually reentered the public mind in part through the influence of Franz Anton Mesmer (1734–1815), who was a lawyer and a self-styled physician of Viennese descent. Mesmer appeared in Paris in 1778, in the decade preceding the French Revolution. He entered into royal courts with this radical theory that all of life was animated by this invisible etheric fluid which he called *animal magnetism*.

Mesmer maintained that if you place an individual into a kind of trance state, what we would call a hypnotic trance—recall Neville talking about this state of drowsiness, this hypnagogic state—you could then realign his or her animal magnetism, this ethereal life fluid, and cure physical or mental diseases, and, according to practitioners, introduce powers such as clairvoyance or the ability to speak in unknown foreign tongues. You could heal. You could empower. You could get at the life stuff of the individual. I was recently in a Walgreen's drugstore and saw an ad reading, "Mysterious and Mesmerizing," for a skin lotion. It's funny how occult language, unmoored from its meaning, lingers in daily life.

Mesmer was feted in royal courts but his philosophy aroused suspicion. At the instigation of King Louis XVI, Mesmerism was discredited by a royal commission in 1784. This investigatory commission was chaired by Benjamin Franklin, who at the time was America's ambassador to France. The commission concluded that there was no such thing as animal magnetism and that whatever cures or effects were experienced under the influence of a mesmeric trance were "in the imagination." But there the committee left dangling its most extraordinary question. If it's "in the imagination," why should there be any effects at all?

Mesmer's greatest students edged away from the idea of animal magnetism as some physical, ethereal fluid. They believed something else was at work. In their struggle for answers, they arrived at the first descriptions of what we would later call subliminal mind and then the subconscious or unconscious mind. Mesmer's proteges did not possess a psychological vocabulary—they preceded and in some regards prefigured modern psychology—but they knew that *something* was evident and effective in his theory of animal magnetism. The best students morphed the master's theories into an early, rough iteration of the subconscious mind. This is an overlooked and crucial basis for the growth of modern psychology. The terms subliminal and subconscious mind began to be heard in the 1890s.

Mesmer died in 1815. But his ideas were taken up in many quarters including, fatefully, by a New England clockmaker named Phineas Quimby (1802–1866). Starting in the late 1830s, Quimby began to experiment with how states of *personal excitement* could make him feel better physically. Quimby suffered from tuberculosis and he discovered that when he would take vigorous carriage rides in the Maine countryside, the effects of tuberculosis would lift. Quimby began to probe the state of his mood and the state of his physical wellbeing. He treated others and became known as a mental healer in the mid-1840s.

At first, Quimby worked with a teenaged boy named Lucius Burkmar. Lucius would enter a trance or hypnagogic state from which he was said to be able to clairvoyantly view people's bodily organs and diagnose and prescribe cures for diseases. Quimby discovered that sometimes the cures that Lucius prescribed, which were often botanical remedies or herbal teas, had previously been prescribed by physicians—and did not work. But when Lucius prescribed them, *they often did work.* The difference, Quimby concluded, was in the *confidence of the patient.* Quimby stopped working with Lucius and encouraged patients to arouse mental energies on their own.

American medicine in the mid-1840s was in a horrendously underdeveloped state. It was the one area of the sciences in which American lagged behind Europe. People had some reason to be driven to mental healers and prayer healers because, if anything, they were less dangerous than most of what was then standard allopathic medicine, which involved measures that were medieval. Physicians were performing bloodletting, administering mercury and other poisons and narcotics. At the very least, the mental healing movement caused no harm.

And, according to historical letters, articles, and diaries, sometimes it did a lot of good. Someone who briefly served as a student to Quimby was Mary Baker Eddy (1821–1910), who founded her own movement called Christian Science. Eddy taught that the healing ministry of Christ is an ever-present fact that is still going on on Earth, and that individuals could be healed by the realization that there is only one true reality and that is this great divine mind that created the universe and that animates everything around us; and further that matter, these forms that we live in, and the floorboards underneath our feet, are not real. They are illusory, as are illness, prejudice, violence, and all human corruption. Eddy taught that through prayer and proper understanding of Scripture, the individual could be healed. She was a remarkable figure. Sometimes people will say, in a far too hasty way, "Well, she took all her ideas from Quimby." It's not that simple. Her interlude with Quimby in the early 1860s was vitally important in her development; but her ideas were uniquely her own. She was an extraordinary figure. I don't think we've taken full measure in this culture of how influential Mary Baker Eddy's ideas have been.

Another figure who become indirectly influential in this healing movement was Emanuel Swedenborg (1688–1772), a Swedish scientist and mystic who worked primarily in the 1700s. Swedenborg's central idea was that the mind is a conduit, a capillary, of cosmic laws, and everything that occurs in the world, including our own thoughts, mirrors events in an invisible world, a spiritual world, which we do not see but always interact with. Everything that men and women do on Earth, Swedenborg taught, is a reflection of something occurring in this unseen world, and our minds are almost like receiving stations, spiritual telegraphs, for messages and ideas from a cosmic plane in which we cannot directly participate but are vitally linked.

Swedenborg was an influence on a Methodist minister named Warren Felt Evans, who was also a contemporary of Quimby's, and who briefly worked with him. Evans wrote a book in 1869 called *The Mental Cure* which was the first book to use the term "new age" in the spiritual sense that it's used today. Evans believed that through prayer, proper direction of thought, use of affirmations, and assumption of a confident mental state, the individual could be cured. *The Mental Cure* is not read anywhere today. Yet it is a surprisingly sprightly book. You'd be surprised. When I first had to read *The Mental Cure* I braced myself but I found that its pages turn quite effortlessly. Evans was a brilliant writer. All of his books are obscure today. But he was a seminal figure in the creation of a positive-thinking movement.

More indirectly, the British poet William Blake also had a certain influence on this movement, and on Neville in particular. Blake believed that humans dwell in this coarse world where we are imprisoned in a fortress of illusions; but the one true mind, the great creative imagination of God, can course through us. We can "cleanse the doors of perception." We can feel the coursing of this great mind within us.

These are some of the same ideas that resounded in Hermeticism. There wasn't a direct connection, necessarily. First of all, there weren't many translations of some of the Hermetic literature, which a man like Blake could likely draw upon. People from different epochs and eras often arrived at these parallel cosmic ideas themselves. When academic writers approach New Thought or the positive-thinking movement, they sometimes make the mistake of conflating it with the idealist philosophy of figures like Berkeley, Kant, Hegel, and later Schopenhauer and Nietzsche. The positive-thinking figures were not directly influenced by the idealists. Those figures and their phraseology are absent in early positive-mind writings. People sometimes make the mistake of not realizing that in a country like America, which was a very agricultural country throughout most of the 19th century, little of this material was directly available.

As an example, consider the Tao Te Ching. This great ancient Chinese work on ethics and philosophy wasn't even translated into English until 1838. In the mid-1840s, there existed four

English-language copies in all of the United States. One was in the library at Harvard, one was in Ralph Waldo Emerson's library which he lent out, and two were in private hands. It wasn't like somebody like Phineas Quimby, the New England clockmaker, who was experimenting with moods and the body, could locate Taoist or Hermetic philosophy, or could even read translations of Hegel. Literacy aside, many of these things weren't accessible. It's a mistake to conclude that because one system of thought mirrors another, that the preceding system is necessarily the birth mother of the later one. In the rural environs of America, many of the positive-mind theorists were independently coming up with these ideas.

Moving into the 20th century, we encounter a figure who directly influenced Neville—French mind theorist Emile Coué (1857–1926). Coué was a largely self-trained hypnotherapist. He died in 1926, but shortly before he died, he made two lecture tours of the United States. Coué was hugely popular in the US and in England. He had a key theory, which rested on the principle that when you enter a sleepy drowsy state, the hypnagogic state, your mind is uniquely supple, suggestible, and powerful. Coué came up with a method to use in conjunction with this state. His system was so simple that critics mocked it. You've probably heard of it. Coué told people to gently repeat the mantra, "Day by day, in every way, I am getting better and better." He said you should lay in bed and recite this just as you're drifting off at night and again just as you're coming to in the morning. Whisper it twenty times to yourself. You could knot a piece of string twenty times and take that piece of string with you, keep it at your bedside, so you could count off your repetitions like a rosary.

Coué had many thousands of followers, but he also became a figure of ridicule because the critics said: "How could such a simple idea possibly do anything for anyone?" Of course, they would not try it. To their minds, it was prima facie nonsense. Such an attitude reminds me of the character of Dr. Zaius from *Planet of the Apes* insisting that flight is a physical impossibility. Thought in the absence of experience is the impoverishment of our intellectual culture. Certainty in the absence of personal experience precludes effort.

In addition to the uses of hypnagogia, another of Coué's ideas appeared in Neville's thought system. You can find the language from time to time in Neville's lectures and writing. That is, within human beings exist two forces: *will* and *imagination*. The *will* is intellectual self-determination. The *imagination* is the mental images and emotionally conditioned reactions that populate our psyches, particularly with regard to self-image. Coué said that when imagination and will are in conflict, *imagination always win*. Your emotional state always overcomes your intellect.

As an example, Coué said, place a wooden plank on the floor and ask an average person to walk across it. He or she will have no problem. But if you raise that same wooden plank twenty feet off the ground, in many cases the person will be petrified even though there's no difference in the physical demand. They are capable of walking across it. The risk of falling is minimal. *The change in condition alone creates an emotional state that makes them more nervous and hence accident prone.* Coué believed it necessary to cultivate new imaginative images of ourselves. We cannot do that through the intellect alone. But we can do so by making using of this very subtle hypnagogic state. He called his method auto-suggestion. It was self-hypnosis essentially. Neville adopted the method, if not the same assumptions behind it.

The Mystic in Life

There are few pictures of Neville. His smiles glowingly in rare pictures toward the end of his life. He died young at age 67 in 1972. He died of heart failure in West Hollywood where he was living with his family. Until the end, his voice and his powers of communication never left him. They absolutely resonated.

It's interesting sometimes to look at the lives of mystical figures like Neville who are hard to pin down, but who did lead domestic lives. There was a little piece in the *Los Angeles Times* on October 21, 1962: "Ms. Goddard Named as College President." It went on, "Miss Victoria Goddard, daughter of Mr. and Mrs. Neville Goddard, has been appointed co-chairman of campus publicity by the student government president at Russell Sage College for New York. She is an English major." This was Neville's daughter.

Now, Victoria Goddard or Vicky as she's known, is still living. She lives in Los Angeles in the family house that she once resided in with her parents. She avoids publicity and contact with people who are interested in Neville's ideas. I've tried to reach out to her but she has no interest in being in touch. She did give her approval indirectly to an anthology of Neville's writings that I wrote an introduction to, but she doesn't want contact with his students. She wants to lead her own existence. But it's funny sometimes we come across little things like this article or a photograph and realize that every one of us share the same workaday concerns.

For all of Neville's wonderful mystical theories, I just have to share this little discourse that he went into about Liquid-Plumr in a lecture that he delivered in 1970. I found this a delightful reminder of how the ordinary steps into all of our lives even when we're trying to deal with cosmic and mystical concerns. He told an audience in 1970:

So you buy something because of highly publicized TV promotions. Someone highly publicized what is called "Liquid-Plumr." And so I had some moment in my bathroom where the sink was all stopped up, so I got the Liquid-Plumr. Poured it in, in abundance. It said it's heavier than water, and it would go all the way down and just eat up everything that is organic and will not hurt anything that is not organic, so I poured it in. Water still remained; it didn't go down. Called the plumber the next day. He couldn't come that day but he would come the next day. So it was forty-eight hours. So when he came the entire sink was eaten away by the Liquid-Plumr. So I asked him: "Does this thing work?" He said: "It does for two people: the one who manufactures it, and the one who sells it." They are the only ones who profit by the Liquid-Plumr. And so you turned on the TV and you saw it and you bought it. It is still on TV and I am sinning, because to sin by silence when I should protest makes cowards of us all. But I haven't protested to the station that advertises this nonsense and I haven't protested to the place where I got it or to anyone who manufactures it, so I am the silent sinner. Multiply me because of my embarrassment. Here is a sink completely eaten up by Liquid-Plumr.

"The silent sinner," he called himself. I lodge letters of protest and phone calls from time to time, so I can sympathize with everything Neville says here.

Neville published a variety of books during his lifetime, most of them quite short. There was a company in Los Angeles called G and J Publishing which issued most of his books. A symbol appeared on most of his covers, which he devised himself. It was a heart with an eye to symbolize eternal vision, inner vision, and it was part of a fruit-bearing tree. As the emotive state of man conceives, so the tree brings forth fruit.

In 1964, Neville published an extremely rare pamphlet called, *He Breaks The Shell*. On its cover you can see a little cherub or angelic figure coming out of a human head. Neville described this mystical experience and said that this is an experience that all of us will have either in this lifetime or another; and that the whole purpose of human existence is to be reborn from your imagination; and your imagination, as we experience it, is physically lodged in your skull, entombed in this kind of a womb. Christ was crucified in Golgotha, place of the skull. Neville believed that we each will be reborn from within our own skull, and that we will have an actual physical experience, maybe in the form of a dream, but a vivid, tactile experience of being reborn from out of the base of our skull. We will know, in that moment, that we are fulfilling our essential purpose.

He described this quite vividly. He had this experience in New York City in 1959 where he had an enormously tactile, sensationally real dream of being reborn from out of the skull. Minerva was said to have been reborn from the skull of Zeus or Jupiter. Christ was crucified at the place of the skull. "You and I," Neville said, "will be reborn from within our skull." In the late 1960s a booking agent told him, "Listen, you've got to stop telling this story at your talks. It's freaking everyone out. People want to hear the get-rich stuff." He told Neville that he if did not change course he'd have no audience left. "Then I'll tell it to the bare walls," Neville replied. He spoke of his mystical experience for the rest of his career until he died in 1972.

I reissued one of Neville's books recently, *The Power of Awareness*. I felt that, for the first time, Neville's books needed to be packaged in a way that fits their dignity, and this is a beautiful edition that I took great joy in working on because I thought it represented him with the right degree of dignity.

I want to quote from Neville's voice. He spoke in such beautiful, resonant language, so unhaltingly, never a pause, never an uncertainty. He knew his outlook so well, he could share it effortlessly. Here is his voice.

> So I'm telling you of the power within you and that power is your own wonderful human imagination. And that is the only God in the world. There is no other God. That is the Jesus Christ of Scripture, so tonight take it seriously. If you really have an objective in this world and you're waiting for something to happen on the outside to make it so, forget it. Do it in your own wonderful human imagination. Actually bring it into being in your own imagination. Conjure a scene which would imply the fulfillment of that dream and lose yourself in the action as you contemplate it, and completely lose yourself in that state. If you're completely absorbed in it, you will objectify it and you will see it seemingly independent of your perception of it. But even if you do not have that intensity, if you lose yourself in it and feel it to true—the imaginal act—then drop it. In a way you do not know, it will become true.

If you are interested in hearing more of Neville, you can go online and find lectures that are posted on YouTube and almost everywhere. He allowed people who came to presentations to tape record them and freely distribute them. He claimed copyright over nothing, and that, to me, is the mark of a real leader. That's the mark of a real thinker. You don't have to join anything. You don't have to ask anybody permission for anything. You don't have to pay any dues. You don't have to buy anything. You just start.

Neville's Circle

I want to say a quick word about some of the people who have been influenced by Neville today. One of them is the major-league baseball pitcher, Barry Zito, who actually introduced me to Neville. I was doing an article about Barry in 2003 and he said to me, "Oh, you must be into Neville," and I said, "I've never heard of him." He said, "Really? You never heard of him?" He was the first one who got me interested in Neville's thought, and that was a huge influence in my life. It was almost 10 years ago to this very day and in many regards put me where I am today.

The New Age writer Wayne Dyer wrote a lot about Neville in his most recent book which is called *Wishes Fulfilled.* But a really remarkable influence that Neville brought into the world came in the form his subtle impact on the writer, Carlos Castaneda, of whom I'm a great admirer. I want to read a short passage from my forthcoming book, *One Simple Idea:*

> By the mid-1950s, Neville's life story exerted a powerful pull on a budding writer whose own memoirs of mystic discovery later made him a near-household name: Carlos Castaneda. Castaneda told his own tales of tutelage under a mysterious instructor, in his case a Native American

sorcerer named Don Juan. Castaneda first discovered Neville through an early love interest in Los Angeles, Margaret Runyan, who was among Neville's most dedicated students. A cousin of American storyteller Damon Runyon, Margaret wooed the stocky Latin art student at a friend's house, slipping Carlos a slender Neville volume called *The Search,* in which she had inscribed her name and phone number. The two became lovers and later husband and wife. Runyan spoke frequently to Castaneda about her mystical teacher Neville, but he responded with little more than mild interest—with one exception.

In her memoirs, Runyan recalled Castaneda growing fascinated when the conversation turned to Neville's discipleship under an exotic teacher. She wrote:

> It was more than the message that attracted Carlos, it was Neville himself. He was so mysterious. Nobody was really sure who he was or where he had come from. There were vague references to Barbados in the West Indies and his being the son of an ultra-rich plantation family, but nobody knew for sure. They couldn't even be sure about this Abdullah business, his Indian teacher, who was always way back there in the jungle, or someplace. The only thing you really knew was that Neville was here and that he might be back next week, but then again . . .

"There was," Runyon concluded, "a certain power in that position, an appealing kind of freedom in the lack of past and Carlos knew it."

Carlos knew it. Both Neville and Castaneda were dealing the same basic idea, and one that has a certain pedigree in America's alternative spiritual culture: tutelage under hidden spiritual masters.

Neville again and again told this story, that there was a turbaned black man of Jewish descent who tutored him starting in 1931 in kabbalah, Scripture, number symbolism, and mental metaphysics. He described Abdullah as this somewhat taciturn, mysterious figure who he met one day at a metaphysical lecture in 1931. Neville walked in and Abdullah said to him, "Neville, you're six months late." Neville said, "I had never seen this man before." Abdullah continued, "The brothers told me you were coming and you're six months late." He said they spent the next five years together studying.

Neville had his first true awakening experience in the winter of 1933. He was dying to get out of the Manhattan winter. He wanted to spend Christmas back home with his family in Barbados. He had no money and Abdullah said to him, "Walk the streets of Manhattan as if you are there and you shall be." And so Neville said he would walk the gray wintry streets of the Upper West Side with the feeling that he was in the palm-lined lanes of Barbados. He would go to see Abdullah, telling him, "It isn't working. I'm still here." And Abdullah would slam the door in his face and say, "You're not here. You're in Barbados."

Then one day, before the last ship departed for Barbados, his brother, Victor, from out of the blue, without any physical intercession on Neville's part, sent him a first-class steamer ticket and $50. "Come spend winter with us in Barbados," he wrote. Neville said he was transformed by the experience. He felt that it was Abdullah's law of mental assumption came to his rescue.

Now, this idea of mysterious spiritual masters got popularized in modern Western culture through the influence of Madame Blavatsky and her partner Colonel Henry Steel Olcott who founded the movement of Theosophy in New York City in 1975. They claimed to be under the tutelage of hidden spiritual masters, Master Koot Hoomi, who was said to be Tibetan, and Master Morya who was said to be Indian. These adepts, they said, would send them phenomenally produced letters, advising them what to do, giving them directions, giving them advice, giving them succor. Around that time, Colonel Olcott and Madame Blavatsky were living in a building which is still standing at the corner of 8th Avenue of West 47th Street which was known as the Lamasery, their headquarters or salon, where they dwelt on the second floor. Today it is an Econo Lodge. None of the people who worked there were very entranced with my attempts to explain the history of the building.

Colonel Olcott said that one time in the winter of 1877, Master Morya materialized in his room and directed him and Madame Blavatsky to relocate to the nation of India, which they did the following year. They helped instigate the Indian independence movement. Olcott went on speaking tours all over the Near East, Far

East, Japan, Sri Lanka. He helped instigate a rebirth of Buddhism throughout the East. Blavatsky and Olcott were enormously effective in their way. Colonel Olcott attributed all of it to the presence of these mysterious spiritual masters, these great turbaned figures somewhere from the East who had given them instruction.

Now, I first wrote about Neville in an article that was published in February 2005 in *Science of Mind* magazine called "Searching for Neville Goddard." Things had been fairly quiet around Neville for many years, and that article attracted a lot of interest. I started receiving phone calls and e-mail after e-mail asking me, who was Abdullah? Did he exist? Could he be identified? I would tell people at the time that I thought Abdullah was a kind of a mythos that Neville might have borrowed, clipped and pasted, from Theosophy. I didn't think there was any evidence to show that Abdullah was a real person, and I thought the dramatic claims around him were probably Neville's mythmaking.

Now, to my surprise, I discovered something about Abdullah through another figure in the positive thinking movement, a man named Joseph Murphy, who died in 1981, and who wrote a very popular book, which some of you may have read, called *The Power of Your Subconscious Mind*. Shortly before his death, Murphy gave a series of interviews to a French-speaking minister from Quebec. The interviewer published his book only in French with Quebec press. It is called *Dialogues with Joseph Murphy* and in these interviews Murphy offhandedly remarks that he, too, was a student of Abdullah. Murphy actually came to New York around the same time as Neville in 1922. He migrated from Ireland. Murphy worked as a pharmacist at the Algonquin Hotel. They used to have a little pharmacy in their lobby. And Murphy also became a metaphysical lecturer and was acquainted with Neville for several years. He stated very simply and matter-of-factly that Abdullah was his teacher too, and that he was a very real man.

I began to look around and correspond with people, and I came to feel, over the past few years, that I happened upon a figure who might actually be Abdullah. He was Arnold Josiah Ford. Ford was a mystic, black nationalist, and part of a movement called the Black Hebrew Movement which still exists in various forms. Ford was born in Barbados, Neville's home island, in 1877. Ford emigrated to Harlem in 1910. He became involved with Marcus Garvey's Universal Negro Improvement Association, of which he was musical director. In surviving photographs Ford, like Abdullah, is turbaned.

In addition to being a dedicated follower of Marcus Garvey— who had his own mind-power metaphysics, about which I'll say a quick word in a moment—Ford was also part of a movement called Ethiopianism. It was a precursor to Rastafarianism. Ford believed, as the Rastafarian people do, as many other people do with good reason, that Ethiopia, one of the oldest continuous civilizations on Earth and one of the most populous nations in Africa, was home to a lost tribe of Israel, which, in this line of teaching, had its own blend of what we know as traditional historical Judaism and mystical teachings and mental metaphysics.

The movement of Ethiopianism believed that this lost African-Israelite tribe harbored a great wealth of ancient teachings that had been lost to most modern people. The Ethiopianism movement believed in mind-power metaphysics and mental healing. Ford was considered a rabbi and he had his own African-American congregation in Harlem. He described himself a man of authentic Israelite and Jewish descent. Writing in 1946, occult philosopher Israel Regardie described Neville's Abdullah as an "Ethiopian rabbi." Regardie, who had been a secretary to the occultist, Aleister Crowley, is quoted on Neville in the introduction.

According to census records, Ford was living in Harlem 1931. He identified his occupation to the census taker as rabbi. That was the same year that Neville met Abdullah. (Although he later gave Abdullah's address as the Upper West Side, not Harlem.) Neville may have been playing around with the name a little bit. He would affectionately refer to Abdullah in his lectures as *Ab*. Ab is a variant of the Hebrew word *abba* for father. Perhaps he saw Abdullah, Ford, as kind of a father figure. He said they studied metaphysics, Scripture, Kabbalah together for five years. Ford has been written about in histories of the Black Hebrew Movement as a key figure who brought authentic knowledge of the Hebrew language, Talmud, and Kabbalah into the Black Hebrew Movement as it existed in Harlem at that time.

Ford was a person of some learning. He was, as I said, a follower of Marcus Garvey, a figure about whom I write in *Occult America*. Garvey has not been properly understood in our culture. He was a pioneering black nationalist figure. He was a great pioneering activist and voice of liberation. He was also very much into his own brand of mental metaphysics. You might recognize this statement of Garvey's which Bob Marley adapted in the lyrics to *Redemption Song:* "We are going to emancipate ourselves from mental slavery because whilst others might free the body, none but ourselves can free the mind." Garvey's speeches are shot through with New Thought language, with the language of mental metaphysics. This was an essential part of Garvey's outlook. This perspective was also essential to the culture of Ethiopianism, which saw Ethiopia's crowned emperor, Haile Selassie, who was coronated in 1930, as a messianic figure. The movement of Ethiopianism morphed into Rastafarianism. It started in the mid-1930s.

Now, there are a lot of correspondences between Arnold Josiah Ford and Neville's description of Abdullah, including physical correspondences, the turban and such. But for all that I've noted, the timeline does not match up sufficiently to make any of this conclusive; because Ford left America sometime in 1931, and he moved to the Ethiopian countryside. After Haile Selassie was coronated as emperor, he offered a land grant to any African-American willing to emigrate to Ethiopia. The emperor saw Ethiopia in a way that matched Ford's ideals as a kind of African-Israel. Haile Selassie wanted Afro-Caribbean and Afro-American people to move, or to come home as he saw it, to Ethiopia, so he offered land grants.

Ford and about thirty followers of Ethiopianism in New York accepted the land grants. There's been some debate about when Ford left, but I have a *New York Times* article that places Ford in New York City still in December 1930. He didn't leave until 1931. That was the same year that Neville said they met. The timeline doesn't match up because Neville said they studied together for five years, so it's possible that Ford was one of several teachers that Neville had, and he created a kind of composite figure who he called Abdullah, Ab, father, of whom Ford may have been a part.

Now, in a coda to Ford's life, I must take note that it was a tougher and braver and more brutal existence back then in some regards. Ford, who for 20 years has been living as a musician and a rabbi in Harlem, moved to rural Ethiopia, the northern part of this nation, to accept Haile Selassie's land grant. He died there in 1935. Tragically, there are no records of Ford's life in Ethiopia. It must have been very difficult. Imagine being a metropolitan person and uprooting yourself to a completely rural setting in a developing nation in the 1930s, and Mussolini is beating the war drum, and Mussolini's fascist troops invaded Ethiopia just weeks after Ford's death, across the north border. This was a man who put himself through tremendous ordeals for his principles. I cannot conclude that Ford was Abdullah. But Murphy's testimony suggests that there *was* an Abdullah, and I think Ford corresponds in many ways—and I write about this in *One Simple Idea*; there probably is some intersection there.

There's another figure I want to mention of a very different kind whose thought had some indirect intersection with Neville's, and that is Aleister Crowley, the British occultist. Crowley made a very interesting statement in a book that he received in a way that we might call channeled perception in 1904; it was later published broadly in 1938 called *The Book of the Law*. In his introduction, Crowley writes:

Each of us has thus an universe of his own, but it is the same universe for each one as soon as it includes all possible experience. This implies the extension of consciousness to include all other consciousnesses. In our present stage, the object that you see is never the same as the one that I see; we infer that it is the same because your experience tallies with mine on so many points that the actual differences of our observation are negligible . . . Yet all the time neither of us can know anything . . . at all beyond the total impression made on our respective minds.

Neville said something similar:

Do you realize that no two people live in the same world? We may be together now in this room, but we will go home tonight and close our doors on entirely different worlds. Tomorrow, we will go to work where we'll meet others but each one of us lives in our own mental and physical world.

Neville meant this in the most literal sense. He believed that every individual, possessed of his or her own imagination, is God, and that everyone you see, including me standing in this room, is rooted in you, as you are ultimately rooted in God.

You exist in this world of infinite possibilities and realities, and that, in fact, when you mentally picture something, you're not creating it—it already exists. You're claiming it. The very fact of being able to experience it mentally confirms that in this world of infinite possibilities, where imagination is the ultimate creative agent, everything that you can picture *already is*.

Mind Science

Some of the things that Neville said prefigured studies both in psychical research and quantum physics. I want to say a quick word about that. One of my heroes is, J.B. Rhine, a psychical researcher who performed tens of thousands of trials at Duke University in the 1930s and beyond to test for clairvoyant perception. Rhine often used a five-suit deck of cards called Zener cards; if you were guessing a card, you had a one-in-five chance, 20 percent, of naming the right card. As Rhine documented in literally tens of thousands of trials, with meticulous clinical control, certain individuals persistently, under controlled conditions, scored higher than a chance hit of 20 percent.

It wasn't always dramatically higher. It wasn't like Zeus was aiming lightning bolts at the Earth. But if someone over the course of thousands of trials keeps scoring 25 percent, 26 percent, 27 percent, beyond all chance possibility, and the results are parsed, juried, gone over, reviewed, you have some anomalous transfer of information going on in a laboratory setting. Rhine's research was real. And Rhine noticed—and he had this quietly monumental way of describing things, he would make some observation in a footnote that could be extraordinary—that the correlation to a high success rate of hits on the Zener cards was usually a feeling of enthusiasm, positive expectation, hopefulness, belief in the possibility of ESP, and an encouraging environment. Then when boredom or physical exhaustion would set in, or interest would wane, the results would go down. If interest was somehow renewed, revised, if there was a feeling of comity in the testing room, the results would go up.

We as a culture haven't begun to deal with the implications of Rhine's experiments. There was another parapsychologist, Charles Honorton, who began a series of experiments in 1970s—I see him as Rhine's successor—called the *ganzfeld* experiments. Ganzfeld is German for whole field. Honorton experimented on subjects who were in a hypnagogic state, the state of drowsiness. Honorton and his collaborators theorized that if you could induce the near-sleep state in an individual, put somebody in conditions of comfortable isolation, fit them with eye coverings and headphones emitting white noise or some kind of negative sound to listen to, put them in a greatly relaxed state, it might be possible to heighten the appearance of some kind of clairvoyant faculty.

His test was to place a subject, a receiver, into a comfortable isolation tank, and to place another subject, a sender, in a different room. Then the sender attempted to mentally convey an image—such as a flower, a rocket, a boat, or something else—to the receiver, and see what happens. These tests generally used four images. Three were decoys, one was actual. Again, in certain subjects, and also in the subjects as a whole in the form of meta-analysis, Honorton found over and over again results that showed a higher than 25 percent chance hit when subjects were placed into the hypnagogic state.

We're in this state all the time. When you're napping, when you're dozing off at your desk, when you're going to sleep at night, when you're waking up in the morning. Neville's message is: *use it.* Honorton died very young in 1992 at age 46. He had suffered health problems his whole life. If he had lived, his name would, I believe, be as well-known as J.B. Rhine. He was a great parapsychologist.

There's another field burgeoning today called neuroplasticity that relates to some of Neville's sights. In short, brain imaging shows that repeat thoughts change the pathways through which electrical impulses travel in your brain. This has been used to treat obsessive compulsive disorder. A research psychologist named Jeffery Schwartz at UCLA has devised a program that ameliorates and dissipates obsessive thoughts. Schwartz's program teaches patients and people in his clinical trials to substitute something in place of an obsessive thought at the very moment they experience it. This diversion may be a pleasurable physical activity, listening to music, jogging, whatever they want, just anything that gets them off that obsessive thought. Schwartz has found through brain imaging, and many scientists have replicated this data, that if you repeat an exercise like that, eventually biologic changes manifest in the brain, neuropathways change, thoughts themselves alter brain biology as far as electrical impulses are concerned.

A New Thought writer in 1911, who theorized without any of the contemporary brain imaging and neuroscience, came up with exactly the same prescription. His name was John Henry Randall. Randall called it *substitution*. His language and the language used today by 21st century researchers in neuroplasticity is extraordinarily similar.

Finally, we have emerging from the field of quantum physics an extraordinary set of questions, which have been coming at us actually for 80-plus years, about the extent to which observation influences the manifestation of subatomic particles. I want to give a very brief example. Basically, quantum physics experiments have shown that if you direct a wave of particles, often in the form of a light wave, at a target system, perhaps a double-slit box or two boxes, the wave of light will collapse into a particle state, it will go from a wave state to a particle state. This occurs when a conscious observer is present or a measurement is occurring. Interference patterns demonstrate that the particle-like properties of wave of light *at one time appeared in both boxes*. Only when someone decided to look or to take a measurement did the particles become localized in one box.

In 1935, physicist Erwin Schrodinger noted that the conclusions of these quantum experiments were so outrageous, were so contrary to all observed experience, that he devised a thought experiment called Schrodinger's Cat in order to highlight this surreality. Schrodinger did not intend his thought experiment to endorse quantum theorizing. He intended it to compel quantum theorists to deal with the ultimate and, what he considered, absurdist conclusions of their theories—theories which have never been overturned, theories which have been affirmed for 80 years. Now, Schrodinger's Cat comes down to this, it can be put this way: You take two boxes. You put a cat into one of the two boxes. You direct a subatomic particle at the boxes. One box is empty, one box holds the cat. Inside the box with the cat is what he called a "diabolical device." This diabolical device trips a beaker of poison when it comes in contact with a subatomic particle, thus killing the cat.

So, you do your experiment. You direct the particle and you go to check the boxes. Which box is the particle in? Is the cat dead? Is the cat alive? The cat is *both*, Schrodinger insisted. It must be *both* because the subatomic particle can be shown to exist in more than one place, in a wave state, until someone checks, and thus localizes it into a particle state, occupying one place. Hence, you must allow for both outcomes—you have a dead/alive cat. That makes no sense. All of lived experience says that you've got two boxes; you've got one cat; the cat's dead if you fired into the box with the cat; or the cat's alive if you fired into the other box. Schrodinger said, "Not so." Interference experiments demonstrate that at one point the subatomic particle was in a *wave state*; it was non-local; it existed only in potential; it existed in both boxes and, given the nature of quantum observation, potentially everywhere. It is only when you go to check and open one of the boxes that the particle becomes localized. *It was in both boxes until a conscious observer made the decision to check.*

A later group of physicists argued there's no doubting Schrodinger's conclusion, and in fact, if you were to check eight hours later, you would not only find a cat that was living/dead, but you would find a living cat that was hungry because it hadn't been fed for eight hours. The timing itself created a past, present, and future for the cat—a reality selected out of infinite possibilities. Schrodinger didn't intend for his thought experiment to affirm this radical departure from reality. He intended it to expose what he considered the absurdist conclusions of quantum physics. But quantum physics data kept mounting and mounting, and Schrodinger's thought experiment became to some physicists a very real illustration of the extraordinary physical impossibilities that we were seeing in the world of quantum physics.

The implication is that we live in a serial universe—that there are infinite realities, whether we experience them or not; and our experience of one of these realties rests on observation. If we can extrapolate from the extraordinary behaviors of subatomic particles, it stands to reason that parallel events and potentials are all are occurring simultaneously. Why don't we experience any of this? Our world is seemingly controlled by Newtonian mechanics. There aren't dead/alive cats. There are singular events. Why don't we experience quantum reality?

Today, a theory that makes the rounds among quantum physicists that when something gets bigger and bigger—remember these experiments are done on subatomic particles, the smallest isolated fragments of matter—when we pull back from a microscopic view of things, we experience what is known as "information leakage." The world gets less and less clear as it gets bigger; as we exit the subatomic level and enter the mechanical level that is familiar, we lose information about what's really going on.

American philosopher William James made the same observation in 1902. James said that when you view an object under a microscope, you're getting so much information; but more and more of that information is lost as you pan back. This is true of all human experience. A cohort of quantum physicists today says the same thing: that the actions of the particle lab are occurring around us always, but we don't know it because we lose information in this coarse physical world that we live in.

Neville said something similar. He said that you radiate the world around you by the persuasiveness of your imagination and feelings. A quantum physicist might call this observation. But in our three-dimensional world, Neville said, time beats so slowly that we do not always observe the relationship between the visible world and our inner nature. You and I can contemplate a desire and become it, but because of the slowness of time, it is easy to forget what we formerly set out to worship or destroy. Quantum physicists speak of "information leakage;" Neville basically spoke of "time leakage." Time moves so slowly for us that we lose the sense of cause and effect.

"Scientists will one day explain why there is a serial universe," Neville said in 1948, "but in practice, how you use the serial universe to change the future is more important."

TRY

I want to leave you with a slogan of an American occultist P.B. Randolph who lived in New York City. He was a man of African-American descent and a tremendously original thinker and mystical experimenter. He died at the young age of 49 in 1875. This was his personal slogan: *TRY*. That's all. *TRY*. This slogan later appeared in letters signed by the spiritual masters Koot Hoomi and Morya, which started reaching Colonel Henry Steel Olcott in 1870s. The first appeared about two months before Randolph's death. The letters used the same slogan: *TRY*.

What you're hearing now is something to try. Neville's challenge was as ultimate as it was simple: "Put my ideas to the test." Prove them to yourself or dismiss them, but what a tragedy would be not to try. It's all so simple.

I want to conclude with words from William Blake, who was one of Neville's key inspirations later in life. Blake described the coarsened world of the senses that we live in. He described such things sometimes in matters of geography. When he would say England, he didn't mean England the nation exactly. He meant the coarse world in which men and women find themselves, the world in which we see so little, and the parameters close in so tightly that we don't know what's really going on. Then the poet would talk about Jerusalem, which he saw as a greater world, as a reality, created through the divine imagination, which runs through all men and women.

I want to close with William Blake's ode "Jerusalem" from 1810. I hope you'll try to hear these words as Neville himself heard them.

> *And did those feet in ancient time*
> *Walk upon Englands mountains green:*

And was the holy Lamb of God,
On Englands pleasant pastures seen!

And did the Countenance Divine,
Shine forth upon our clouded hills?
And was Jerusalem builded here,
Among these dark Satanic Mills?

Bring me my Bow of burning gold:
Bring me my arrows of desire:
Bring me my Spear: O clouds unfold!
Bring me my Chariot of fire!

I will not cease from Mental Fight,
Nor shall my sword sleep in my hand:
Till we have built Jerusalem,
In Englands green & pleasant Land.

Questions and Answers

If there are a few questions, I'd be happy to take them.

Speaker: Can you do multiple wishes, say if there are three that you wish?

Mitch: Neville's own students in his lifetime asked him that very thing, and I'm in the same place myself because it's hard sometimes to limit one's wishes to one thing. Neville felt it was more effective if you limit it to one thing at a time; but he said that this was by no means a limit, you didn't have to limit yourself. The key thing is to feel the desire intensely and to hold your mental emotive picture with clarity and simplicity, and to stick with it. He did say he felt that at the time interval would be lessened if you limit yourself to one thing at a time. That was his practice, but he did not call it a must.

Speaker: I wanted something that didn't last, so to try to achieve that, do I meditate on it? How do I get result?

Mitch: Neville's idea was to enact a scene that would naturally transpire when the desired thing comes to pass. There may be many events that would transpire if that thing came to pass, but he said to select just one that has a particular emotional resonance, and then see yourself doing it over and over. Something as simple as a handshake or climbing a ladder. Just take one that has act emotional gravity and be persistent.

Speaker: Do you think that given his predilection for inner vision that there's any evidence suggest that Abdullah may have been a channel? Abdullah may have been a channel or a channel within Neville?

Mitch: Oh, that's an interesting question. He always referred to Abdullah as a flesh-and-blood figure, and he said Abdullah lived in an apartment on West 72nd Street, which I've visited, and he would talk about Abdullah in very physical, vivid terms, so he certainly described him as a flesh-and-blood being.

Speaker: You described many of the techniques, including the technique of walking in a cold winter day to get the feeling of being in another place. This is just other technique for the astral body. Basically, what he's describing is the emotional astral body being developed, of which one expression would be manifesting that state here, but it sounds like he could easily develop another technique because this sounds very limited.

Mitch: He does represent techniques such as walking and imagining himself in the palm tree-lined lanes in Barbados; but he most often came back to this idea of physical immobility and the uses of a hypnagogic state, that drowsy state. He again and again said that others can experiment, and should experiment, but that he personally found that to be the simplest and the most effective method. He would say sometimes he would enter the hypnagogic state and just feel thankful or try to seize upon one expression like *it is wonderful*. He might do that if he didn't have a specific thing that he was longing for at that moment. So he did experiment with some other techniques and points of view. He did said one lecture, "You praise others and you will shine," because it was very important to try to use these techniques to the benefit of another person. For example, if you have a friend who's looking for a job, you might form the mental picture of congratulating him or her on finding the perfect job because Neville believed in the oneness of humanity in the absolute most literal sense. There was no sentimentality about it. He felt that every individual was God.

Speaker: Did he say that he believed that the universe is holographic?

Mitch: He would say, and again, he sometimes made statements more in passing than full on, but he would say explicitly that we live in a universe of infinite possibilities, and everything that you desire, by the very fact of desiring it, because your imagination is a creative agent, already exists. It is a question of just claiming it, which is why it's so important to think from the desire fulfilled. It doesn't matter if you open your eyes or your checkbook or anything else and, of course, reality as we presently know it comes rushing back in. You must continue to think from the wish fulfilled, which he said was tantamount to selecting a reality that already existed. Schrodinger said there's a dead/alive cat. Neville would have said there are infinite outcomes and they all exist.

Speaker: Regarding the slowness of time, I'm curious what his thoughts were as far as the timetables for his technique.

Mitch: He said that we experience definite time intervals and that a time interval is part of the nature of our existence. I may want a new house and I may want that house right now, and I may think from the end of having that house, but he said, in effect, "The fact of the world that we experience here and now is that the trees have to grow to produce wood. The wood has to be harvested and the carpenter has to cut it. There will be time intervals." And he would say, "Your time interval could be an hour, it could be a month, it could be weeks, it could be years." There is a time interval. You nonetheless must stick to the ideal and try to make it just exquisitely effortless. He didn't endorse using the will. This isn't about saying, "I'm going to think this way." It is going into this meditative or drowsy or hypnagogic state, picturing something that confirms the realization of your desire, and feeling it emotionally; he said that when the method fails maybe it's because you're trying too hard. Neville wanted people to understand that there is an exquisite ease that one should feel with exercises.

Speaker: It sounds like he's saying that an emphasis on pure will would upset that balance.

Mitch: Yes. He used the word receptivity and he used the term time interval.

Speaker: Did Neville ever include other ideas outside of his system?

Mitch: He made very few references to other thought systems. He would frequently quote Scripture, mostly the New Testament. He felt the New Testament was a great blueprint and metaphor for human development in the figure of Christ. He felt that the Old Testament was suggestive of the promise and the New Testament was fulfilling of the promise, and beyond that he made little reference to other thought systems. He was chiefly interested in Scripture. He would talk about numbers; he loved symbolism. In his book *Your Faith Is Your Fortune* he talked about certain aspects of the zodiac, astrology, and number symbolism; but as time passed, he made fewer references to other systems. Every now and again he'd use a piece of language where I'll detect Emile Coué echoed; but so much of what we talked about really came from his own description of the world through his own experience. He made little reference to other systems.

Speaker: I started reading your book *Occult America* and there was a question in my mind—you write that a lot of positive thinkers and people in New Age in American history have, on the one hand, kind of advocated basic techniques and methods for self-ish success and money, and, on the other hand, a lot of the better writers in New Age and New Thought were passionately involved with and concerned about social movements. Where did Neville fall in that dichotomy?

Mitch: That's a wonderful question and that was an aspect for me that made it difficult to first enter Neville's work, because he had no social concerns in the conventional sense, and if people raised social concerns, he would push them aside and would insist that the world you see, whether it is of beauty or violence, is self-created. Prove the theory to yourself and then use the theory as you wish. You want to eliminate suffering? Eliminate suffering. But he ardently rejected fealty to any kind of social movement or ideal. He believed that coming into one's awareness of the godlike nature of imagination, of the literal God presence of the imagina-tion, of having the experience of being reborn through one's skull, was the essential human task.

Speaker: As you said in your own book, a lot the 19th century Spiritualists were involved in movements like suffragism and abolitionism.

Mitch: Yes. Well, you know, these radical movements, radical political movements and radical spiritual movements, avant-garde politics, avant-garde spirituality, they all intersect. We often fail to understand how a figure like Marcus Garvey, for example, was involved with mental metaphysics; but as you get closer to the real lives of these people, the connection becomes more natural because they craved a new social order both spiritually and socially.

A Neville Goddard Timeline

1905: Neville Lancelot Goddard is born on February 19 to a British family in St. Michael, Barbados, the fourth child in a family of nine boys and one girl.

1922: At age seventeen Neville relocates to New York City to study theater. He makes a career as an actor and dancer on stage and silent screen, landing roles on Broadway, silent film, and touring Europe as part of a dance troupe.

1923: Neville briefly marries Mildred Mary Hughes, with whom he has a son, Joseph Goddard, born the following year.

1929: Neville marked this as the year that begin his mystical journey: "Early in the morning, maybe about three-thirty or four o'clock, I was taken in spirit into the Divine Council where the gods hold converse." (lecture from *Immortal Man*, 1977)

1931: After several years of occult study, Neville meets his teacher Abdullah, a turbaned black man of Jewish descent. The pair work together for five years in New York City.

1938: Neville begins his own teaching and speaking.

1939: Neville's first book, *At Your Command*, is published.

1940–1941: Neville meets Catherine Willa Van Schumus, who is to become his second wife.

1941: Neville publishes his longer and more ambitious book, *Your Faith Is Your Fortune*.

1942: Neville marries Catherine, who later that year gives birth to their daughter Victoria. Also that year, Neville publishes *Freedom for All: A Practical Application of the Bible*.

1942–1943: From November to March, Neville serves in the military before returning home to Greenwich Village in New York City. In 1943, Neville is profiled in *The New Yorker*.

1944: Neville publishes *Feeling Is the Secret*.

1945: Neville publishes *Prayer: The Art of Believing*.

1946: Neville meets mystical philosopher Israel Regardie in New York, who profiles him in his book *The Romance of Metaphysics*. Neville also publishes his pamphlet *The Search*.

1948: Neville delivers his classic "Five Lessons" lectures in Los Angeles, which many students find the clearest and most compelling summation of his methodology. It appears posthumously as a book.

1949: Neville publishes *Out of This World: Thinking Fourth Dimensionally*.

1952: Neville publishes *The Power of Awareness*.

1954: Neville publishes *Awakened Imagination*.

1955: Neville hosts radio and television shows in Los Angeles.

1956: Neville publishes *Seedtime and Harvest: A Mystical View of the Scriptures*.

1959: Neville undergoes the mystical experience of being reborn from his own skull. Other mystical experiences follow into the following year.

1960: Neville releases a spoken-word album.

1961: Neville publishes *The Law and Promise*; the final chapter, "The Promise," details the mystical experience he underwent in 1959, and others that followed.

1964: Neville publishes the pamphlet *He Breaks the Shell: A Lesson in Scripture*.

1966: Neville publishes his last full-length book, *Resurrection*, composed of four works from the 1940s and the contemporaneous closing title essay, which outlines the fullness of his mystical vision and of humanity's realization of its deific nature.

1972: Neville dies in West Hollywood at age 67 on October 1, 1972 from an "apparent heart attack" reports the *Los Angeles Times*. He is buried at the family plot in St. Michael, Barbados.

About the Authors

NEVILLE GODDARD was one of the most remarkable mystical thinkers of the past century. In more than ten books and thousands of lectures, Neville, under his solitary first name, expanded on one core principle: *the human imagination is God.* As such, he taught, everything that you experience results from your thoughts and feeling states. Born to an Anglican family in Barbados in 1905, Neville travelled to New York City at age seventeen in 1922 to study theater. Although he won roles on Broadway, in silent films, and toured internationally with a dance troupe, Neville abandoned acting in the early 1930s to dedicate himself to metaphysical studies and embark a new career as a writer and lecturer. He was a compelling presence at metaphysical churches, spiritual centers, and auditoriums until his death in West Hollywood, California, in 1972. Neville was not widely known during his lifetime, but today his books and lectures have attained new popularity. Neville's principles about the creative properties of the mind prefigured some of today's most radical quantum theorizing, and have influenced several major spiritual writers, including Carlos Castaneda and Joseph Murphy.

MITCH HOROWITZ is a PEN Award-winning historian whose books include *Occult America, One Simple Idea, The Miracle Club,* and *The Miracle Habits*. His book *Awakened Mind* is one of the first works of New Thought translated and published in Arabic. The Chinese government has censored his work.

Twitter: @MitchHorowitz

Instagram: @MitchHorowitz23

Printed in the USA
CPSIA information can be obtained
at www.ICGtesting.com
JSHW012036140824
68134JS00033B/3082